A VOYAGE ROUND MY FATHER

John Mortimer's father was a barrister who suddenly became blind when his son was still a small boy, but who carried on with his practice – and his life – as if nothing had happened. *A Voyage Round My Father*, a remarkable essay in direct autobiography on the stage, presents both a portrait of the playwright's father and a dramatization of his own relationship with him – over a period of some twenty years. Originally performed at Greenwich in 1970, the play was staged at the Haymarket Theatre in August 1971.

'The play's style is an expression of the father's. He deals with his disability by a combination of stoic dismissal and Edwardian frivolity . . . His jokes and stories are the public face of a very private man, whose privacy Mortimer respects, and it is that chosen persona, clownish, dignified, amusing and amused, which Mortimer celebrates lovingly. It's one of the best things he's written.' Ronald Bryden on the 1970 production.

A VOYAGE ROUND MY FATHER

John Mortimer

METHUEN & CO LTD
11 NEW FETTER LANE LONDON EC4

First published in 1971
by Methuen & Co Ltd
Copyright © 1971 by Advanpress Ltd
Printed in Great Britain
by Cox & Wyman Ltd
Fakenham Norfolk
SBN 416 66780 5 Hardback
416 66790 2 Paperback

The first version of *A Voyage Round My Father* was presented at the Greenwich Theatre in 1970. This final version of the play was first presented at the Haymarket Theatre in August 1971 with the following cast:

FATHER	*Alec Guinness*
MOTHER	*Leueen MacGrath*
SON (*grown up*)	*Jeremy Brett*
ELIZABETH	*Nicola Pagett*
SON (*as a boy*)	
FIRST BOY	*Jason Kemp*
REIGATE	
SECOND BOY	*Jeremy Burring*
IRIS	
GIRL	*Melanie Wallace*
HEADMASTER	
GEORGE	*Jack May*
HAM	
BOUSTEAD	
SPARKS	*Mark Kingston*
MR MORROW	
LADY VISITOR	
MATRON	
MISS COX	*Phyllida Law*
DORIS	
SOCIAL WORKER	
MRS REIGATE	
MISS BAKER	
FIRST ATS GIRL	*Rhoda Lewis*
WITNESS	
RINGER LEAN	
MR THONG	*Andrew Sachs*
FILM DIRECTOR	

JAPHET
FIRST JUDGE
SECOND JUDGE   *Richard Fraser*
CHIPPY
DOCTOR
SECOND ATS GIRL   *Tilly Tremayne*
REIGATE'S FATHER
ROBING ROOM MAN

Directed by Ronald Eyre

ACT ONE

The stage is bare except for a table and three chairs, downstage left, which are either indoor or outdoor furniture, and a bench downstage right. There is also some foliage downstage, suggestive of a garden: in particular, inverted flowerpots on sticks to act as earwig traps. This setting is permanent: changes of lighting only indicate the changes of place. The FATHER *and the* SON *(grown up) enter.*

FATHER. Roses . . . not much of a show of roses.

SON (*grown up*). Not bad.

FATHER. Onions . . . hardly a bumper crop would you say?

SON (*grown up*). I suppose not.

> *The* FATHER, *a man in his sixties, wearing a darned tweed suit, a damaged straw hat and carrying a clouded malacca walking stick is, with blind eyes, inspecting his garden. His hand is on the arm of the* SON. *They move together about the garden during the following dialogue.*

FATHER. Earwigs at the dahlias. You remember, when you were a boy, you remember our great slaughter of earwigs?

SON. I remember.

FATHER. You see the dahlias?

SON. Yes.

FATHER. Describe them for me. Paint me the picture . . .

SON. Well, they're red . . . and yellow. And blowsy . . .

FATHER (*puzzled*). Blowsy?

SON. They look sort of over-ripe. Middle-aged . . .

FATHER. Earwig traps in place, are they?

SON. They're in place.

> *He leaves the* FATHER, *fetches a camp stool, puts it up, guides the* FATHER *to sit down on it beside a plant.*

FATHER. When you were a boy, we often bagged a hundred ear-wigs in a single foray! Do you remember?

SON. I remember.

> *The* SON *moves away from the* FATHER *and speaks to the audience.*

My father wasn't always blind . . .

> *The* FATHER *starts to tie up the plant, expertly and with neat fingers. He can obviously see.*

The three of us lived in a small house surrounded, as if for protection, by an enormous garden.

> *The* MOTHER *enters carrying a camp stool. She puts it down beside the* FATHER *and starts to help him tie up the plant.*

He was driven to the station, where he caught a train to London and the Law Courts, to his work as a barrister in a great hearse-like motor which he would no more have thought of replacing every year than he would have accepted a different kind of suit or a new gardening hat. As soon as possible he returned to the safety of the dahlias, the ritual of the evening earwig hunt.

> *A* LADY VISITOR *appears on the side of the stage, waves to the* FATHER *who goes into hiding, moving his stool behind the plant he is tending, peers out anxiously.*

SON. Visitors were rare and, if spotted – calling from the gate – my father would move deeper into the foliage until the danger was past.

> *The* LADY VISITOR, *frustrated, withdraws. During the following speech, the* FATHER *moves his stool back into its former position.*

Those were the days when my father could see . . . before I went away to school. When it was always a hot afternoon and a girl called Iris taught me to whistle.

FATHER. Where's the boy got to?

MOTHER. Disappeared, apparently.

The SON *(as a boy) and a small girl,* IRIS, *come running on chasing each other. In a corner the* SON *(as a boy) kneels in front of* IRIS *who is sitting neatly as she gives him a whistling lesson. The boy is blowing but no sound emerges.*

FATHER. He's running wild!

IRIS. Stick out your lips. Stick them out far. Go on. Further than that. Much further. Now blow. Not too hard. Blow gently. Gently now. Don't laugh. Take it seriously. Blow!

Sound of a whistle.

BOY. What was that?

IRIS. What do you mean – what was that?

BOY. Someone whistled.

IRIS. It was you.

BOY. Me?

IRIS. It was you whistling!

BOY. I can do it! I know how to do it!

IRIS. Well, you've learnt something . . .

FATHER. I said – the boy's probably running wild.

MOTHER. Oh, I don't think so.

In his corner with IRIS *the* BOY *manages another whistle. They chatter quietly together during the following scene.*

FATHER. Oh yes he is. And a good thing too. When I was a young boy in Africa, they sent me off – all by myself – to a small hotel up country to run wild for three months. I took my birthday cake with me and kept it under my bed. I well remember . . . (*He laughs.*) . . when my birthday came round I took the cake out, sat on my bed, and ate it. That was my celebration!

MOTHER. He'll soon be going away to school . . .

FATHER. What did you say?

MOTHER. He'll be going away to school . . . We can't expect him to stay here . . . for ever . . .

She gets up, folds her camp stool and leaves with it.
A light change. Bright sun through leaves. The FATHER *gets a step ladder and starts to walk up it, singing to himself.*

FATHER (*singing*).
  'She was as bee . . . eautiful as a butterfly
  And as proud as a queen
  Was pretty little Polly Perkins of Paddington
  Green . . .'

SON (*grown up*). One day he bought a ladder for pruning the apple trees. He hit his head on the branch of a tree and the retinas left the balls of his eyes.

Sudden, total BLACKOUT *in which we hear the* SON'S *voice.*

SON'S VOICE (*grown up*). That's the way I looked to my father from childhood upwards. That's how my wife and his grand-children looked . . . My father was blind but we never mentioned it.

The lights fade up slowly to reveal the FATHER, MOTHER, *and* SON *(as a boy sitting round a breakfast table. The* FATHER *is clearly totally blind, the* MOTHER *is helping him cut up his toast, guiding his hand as he eats a boiled egg.*

SON (*grown up*). He had a great disinclination to mention anything unpleasant. What was that? Courage, cowardice, indifference or caring too completely? Why didn't he blaspheme, beat his brains against the pitch black sitting room walls? Why didn't he curse God? He had a great capacity for rage – but never at the Universe.

The SON *(grown up) goes. The family eat in silence until the* FATHER *suddenly bursts out.*

FATHER. Take it away! This plate's stone cold! My egg! It's

bloody runny! It's in a nauseating condition! What do you want
to do? Choke me to death? (*shouts*) Have you all gone *mad*?
Am I totally surrounded by *cretins*?

Another silence while they go on eating.

FATHER (*singing*).

> 'He asked her for to marry him
> She said "You're very kind"
> But to marry of a milkman
> She didn't feel inclined.
> But when she got married,
> That hard-hearted girl,
> It wasn't to a Viscount,
> It wasn't to an Earl,
> It wasn't to a Marquis,
> But a shade or two WUS!
> 'Twas to the bow-legged conductor
> Of a twopenny bus!'

MOTHER. Marmalade, dear?
FATHER. Thank you.

Silence.

The evolution of the horse was certainly a most tortuous pro-
cess. None of your seven day nonsense! Seven days' labour
wouldn't evolve one primitive earth worm.

Nobody says anything.

FATHER (*singing very loudly*).

> 'She was as beautiful as a butterfly,
>   and as proud as a queen
> Was pretty little Polly Perkins of
>   Paddington Green!'

Silence.

Is the boy still here?

MOTHER. Please, dear. Don't be tactless . . .

FATHER. I thought he'd gone away to school.

MOTHER. *Pas avant le garçon.*

FATHER. What?

MOTHER. He doesn't like it mentioned.

FATHER. Well he's either going away or he's not. I'm entitled to know. If he's here this evening he can help me out with the earwigs.

MOTHER (*confidential whisper to the* FATHER). Mr Lean's going to drive him. A trois heures et demi.

FATHER. Half past three, eh?

MOTHER. Yes, dear. Mr. Lean's going to drive him.

FATHER (*to* BOY). You'll learn to construct an equilateral triangle and the Latin word for parsley. Totally useless information . . .

MOTHER. We really ought not to depress the boy. (*to* SON) You'll find the French very useful.

FATHER. What on earth for?

MOTHER. Going to France.

FATHER. What's he want to go to France for? There's plenty to do in the garden.

As she guides his hand to the coffee.

The coffee's frozen! (*Drinks.*) Like arctic mud!

MOTHER, *takes no notice, pours him some more coffee, meanwhile trying to cheer the* BOY *up.*

MOTHER. The school's very modern. It seems that some of the older boys do sketching at weekends. From nature! I used to bicycle out with my sketching pad, from the college of art . . . I enjoyed it so much.

FATHER. All education's perfectly useless. But it fills in the *time*! The boy can't sit around here all day until he gets old enough for marriage. He can't sit around – doing the crossword.

MOTHER (*laughing*). Married! Plenty of time to think of that when he's learned to keep his bedroom tidy. (*Pause.*) The headmaster seemed rather charming.

FATHER. No one ever got a word of sense out of a schoolmaster! If they *knew* anything they'd be out doing it. (*to the* BOY.) That'll be your misfortune for the next ten years. To be constantly rubbing up against second rate minds.

MOTHER. At the start of each term apparently the new boys get a little speech of welcome.

FATHER. Ignore that! Particularly if they offer you advice on the subject of life. At a pinch you may take their word on equilateral hexagons . . . but remember! Life's a closed book to schoolmasters.

MOTHER. We'll finish your trunk this afternoon.

FATHER. You won't expect any advice from me, will you? All advice's perfectly useless . . .

MOTHER. I've still got to mark your hockey stick.

FATHER. You're alone in the world, remember. No one can tell you what to do about it.

The BOY *starts to cry.*

What's the matter with the boy?

MOTHER (*apparently incredulous*). He's not crying!

FATHER (*coming out with some advice at last*). Say the word 'rats'. No one can cry when they're saying the word 'rats'. (*Pause.*) It has to do with the muscles of the face.

BOY (*trying to stop himself crying*). Rats.

The lights fade on the breakfast table. The FATHER, MOTHER *and* BOY *go. The* SON (*grown up*) *comes to the edge of the stage.*

SON (*grown up*). Mr Ringer Lean was an ex-jockey who drove my father's antique Morris Oxford. He treated it as though it were a nervous stallion.

RINGER LEAN *enters downstage right, carrying a school trunk on his shoulder.*

RINGER. Car's lazy today. Going don't suit her. Shit scared are you? Being sent away . . .

The SON *(as a boy) comes on to the stage. He is wearing school uniform, carrying a suitcase and looking extremely depressed.*

SON *(grown up)*. I was to be prepared for life. Complete with house shoes, gym shoes, football boots, shirts grey, shirts white, Bulldog Drummond, mint humbugs, boxing gloves, sponge bags, and my seating plans for all the London Theatres . . .

BOY. Yes.

He puts down the trunk, rests on it.

RINGER. They sent me away when I was your age. Newmarket Heath. Bound as a stable lad. Bloody terrified I was, at your age . . .

BOY. Were you?

RINGER. They shouldn't send you away. You're going to develop too tall for a jockey.

BOY. I don't think they want me to be a jockey . . .

RINGER. Broke a few bones, I did – first they sent me away. Ribs fractured. Collar bone smashed. Pelvis pounded to pieces. Bad mounts . . . Bad Governors . . . When a Governor gets after you, you want to know . . .

BOY. What?

RINGER. Get to the hay loft, and pull the ladder up after you. They can't climb. Recall that. Governors can't climb. Often I've hid up the hay loft one, two, three hours sometimes. Till the Governor got a winner, and change of heart. Slept up there often. All right when the rats don't nip you.

BOY. Thanks.

RINGER. Only advice I got to give you . . . never avoid a mount. Lad at our stable avoided a half broken two year old. Nasty tempered one with a duff eye. This lad was so shit scared to ride it, that you know what he did?

BOY. No . . .

RINGER. Nobbled himself with a blunt razor blade. Severed a tendon. Then gangrene. Lad had to kiss his leg goodbye.

> RINGER LEAN *picks up the trunk. He and the* SON (*as a boy*) *walk off down stage left.*

> *The light changes, coming up upstage where the* HEADMASTER, *with long white hair, a gown and a stiff collar, is standing ready to address the boys – beside him is the school* MATRON *in uniform, and a young master,* JAPHET, *with a tie tied in a wide knot and an elegant, man-of-the world appearance.*

> RINGER LEAN *and the* SON (*as a boy*) *re-enter downstage right with luggage, and cross the stage.*

BOY. It's not really a stable . . .

RINGER. So never try and nobble yourself. That's my advice. Or sterilize the blade. Hold it in a flame. Kill the germs on it!

BOY. It's more a school than a stable . . .

RINGER. Wherever there's lads, I expect it's much the same . . .

SON (*grown up*). My father had warned me – But this was a great deal worse than I'd expected.

> RINGER LEAN *and the* SON (*as a boy*) *go off.*

HEADMASTER. Now, new boys. Stand up now. Let me look at you. Some day, some long distant day, you will be one yearers, and then two yearers, and then three yearers. You will go away, and you will write letters, and I shall try hard to remember you. Then you'll be old boys. Old Cliffhangers. O.C.'s you shall become, and the fruit of your loins shall attend the School by the Water. Leave the room the boy who laughed. The fruit of your loins shall return and stand here, even as you stand here. And we shall teach them. We shall give them sound advice. So the hungry generations of boys shall learn not to eat peas with their knives, or butter their hair, or clean their finger nails with bus tickets. You shall be taught to wash and bowl straight and wipe your dirty noses. When you are in the sixth form you shall see something of golf. You will look on the staff as your friends. At all times you will call us by nick-names. I am Noah. My wife is Mrs Noah. You are the animals. My son Lance is Shem. Mr Pearce and Mr Box are Ham and Japhet. Matey is Matey. Mr Bingo Ollard is Mr Bingo Ollard. These mysteries have I expounded to you, oh litter of runts.

Pause. The lights change as the HEADMASTER, MATEY *and* JAPHET *leave.* HAM *moves to where a blackboard and a desk are set at a corner of the stage, together with two classroom chairs. He starts drawing a right-angled triangle on the blackboard.*

SON (*grown up, to the audience*). The masters who taught us still suffered from shell shock and battle fatigue. Some had shrapnel lodged in their bodies and the classroom would turn, only too easily, into another Passchendaele.

The SON (*as a boy*) *and another boy of his own age, named* REIGATE, *cross the stage and sit on the chairs in front of* HAM'S *blackboard, watching him complete his drawing of Pythagoras' theorem.*

HAM. The square on the longest side of a right angled bloody triangle is . . . is what, Boy?

Standing up in front of the desk, the BOY *says.*

BOY. I don't know . . .

HAM (*suddenly yells*). Straff you, Boy. Bomb and howitzer and straff the living daylights out of you. God bomb you to hell!

HAM *picks up the first pile of books and starts to throw them at the* BOY *one by one, shouting.*

Get your tin hat on . . . ! It's coming over now! (*Throws a book.*) It's equal to the square . . . What square, you unfortunate

cretin?! (*Throws a book.*) On the other two sides. (*Throws a book.*)
Right angled triangle! (*Throws a book.*) All night. Straff you all
night. (*Throws a book.*) Shell and howitzer you! (*Throws a book.*)
Bomb you to hell!

Throws a duster. He sits down, suddenly deflated. Smiles ner-
vously and gets out a small cash book.

All right. All right. War's over . . . Armistice day. **Demob. I**
suppose you want . . . compensation?

BOY. If you like, sir.

HAM. How many books did I throw?

BOY. Six, sir. Not counting the duster.

HAM. Threepence a book and say a penny the duster. Is that fair?

BOY. I'd say so, sir.

HAM. Is that one and six?

BOY. I think it's one and sevenpence, sir.

SON (*grown up*). From Ham I learnt the healing power of money . .

At one side of the stage, sitting on a bench, robed in his wig and
gown and carrying his walking stick, the FATHER *is lit dictating*
a letter to the MOTHER *who, wearing a hat, is sitting beside him.*
The FATHER *speaks as* HAM *puts his hand in his pocket, pulls*
out money and counts it out and gives it to the SON.

FATHER. I am writing to you waiting outside the President's
Court to start a Divorce Case. Like all divorce cases, this one is
concerned with sex, which you will find to be a subject filled
with comic relief. The best part of divorce is that it is filled with
comic relief . . .

JAPHET, strumming a ukelele, appears upstage. The BOY,
having collected his money, moves from the class towards
JAPHET. HAM *and* REIGATE *go off in different directions.*

FATHER. Pearson Dupray, K.C. who is agin me in this case is not
a foeman worthy of my steel. He will no doubt fumble his cross
examination and may even fail to prove my adultery . . . although
God knows . . . I have had inclination and opportunity to spare.

B

JAPHET starts to sing softly to his ukelele.

JAPHET (*sings*).

> 'Hallelujah I'm a bum
> Hallelujah Bum again
> Hallelujah gives us a hand out . . .
> To revive us again . . .'

FATHER. Like you, I shall today be rubbing up against a second rate mind . . .

The SON (as a boy) comes up to JAPHET just as JAPHET is starting the chorus again. The FATHER and MOTHER remain seated on their bench during the following scene.

SON (*grown up*). Japhet, the second master, did his unsuccessful best to impart polish.

JAPHET (*sings*). 'Hallelujah . . . I'm a bum . . .'
    You know what a bum is?

BOY. Yes, sir.

JAPHET (*sings*).

> 'Hallelujah. Bum again . . .
> Hallelujah, gives us a hand out . . .'

Look. No one's going to laugh if you do three simple chords. See? Three simple chords. Like this. Always. For every tune. Take my advice, and look as if you know what you're doing. No one's going to laugh. (*Looks at the* BOY.) You don't tie that tie of yours properly. Remind me to teach you to tie your tie. (*He plays a chord on the ukelele.*) Take my tip, sing in the back of your nose – so it sounds as if you'd crossed the States by railroad . . . (*He starts to sing through his nose to the ukelele.*)

JAPHET (*sings*).

> 'Why don't you go to work
> Like all the other men do?
> How the hell are we going to work
> When there's no fit work to do . . .?
> Hallelujah. I'm a bum!'

Just three simple chords. Don't get ambitious.

BOY. No, I won't, sir.

JAPHET. And remember about your tie. Twice over and then up. That way you get the big knot. Like HE wears it.

BOY. He?

JAPHET. The King, of course.

BOY. Oh yes, sir – of course.

JAPHET. The King and I – we've got a lot in common.

BOY. Yes, sir.

JAPHET. Same tie . . . same trouble.

BOY. What trouble's that, sir?

JAPHET. Woman trouble . . . Deep, deep trouble. Just like the jolly old King . . .

JAPHET *goes sadly, carrying his ukelele. The* BOY *takes a letter out of his pocket, reads it.*

SON (*grown up*). I knew what he was talking about. He was talking about Lydia, a pale red headed girl who smelt vaguely of moth balls and who made our beds. The King and Japhet were tussling with the problems from which my father made his living.

FATHER (*dictating to the* MOTHER). You will be pleased to hear that I won Jimpson v. Jimpson, the wife being found guilty of infidelity in the front of a Daimler parked in Hampstead Garden Suburb. A vital part of the evidence consisted of footprints on the dashboard . . .

MOTHER. Is that really suitable?

FATHER (*ignoring her*). Footprints on the dashboard!

REIGATE *comes in, bored, his hands in his pockets, and wanders near the* BOY. *The* BOY *reading the letter doesn't notice him.*

FATHER. The co-respondent was condemned in costs. My final speech lasted two hours and I made several jokes. At home we have been pricking out Korean chrysanthemums and making marmalade. Unusually large plague of earwigs this year . . .

REIGATE (*to the* BOY). Do you get many letters from home?

The FATHER *and* MOTHER *get up and the* MOTHER *leads the* FATHER *out.*

The BOY *puts the letter hurriedly back in the envelope.*

BOY. Hullo, Reigate. Once a week, I expect . . .

REIGATE. Keep the envelopes . . .

BOY. For the stamps . . .?

REIGATE. To put the fish in, on Sunday nights. The fish is disgusting. Put it in envelopes and post it down the bogs.

BOY. Why in envelopes?

REIGATE. Well you just can't put bits of fish, not straight in your pocket.

Pause.

Is your mother slim?

BOY. Fairly slim.

Pause. REIGATE *takes out a yo-yo and starts to play with it.*

REIGATE. Is your father good at golf?

BOY. Pretty good.

REIGATE (*winding up the string of his yo-yo and putting it away in his pocket*). My mother's slim as a bluebell.

BOY. Well, mine's quite slim too really. She goes to cocktail parties.

REIGATE. Slim as a bluebell! With yellow eyes.

BOY. Yellow?

REIGATE. Like a panther.

BOY. Oh, I see.

REIGATE. Very small feet. High heels of course. Does your mother wear high heels?

BOY. Whenever she goes to cocktail parties. She wears them then.

REIGATE. My mother wears high heels. *Even at breakfast.* Of course she's slim as a bluebell . . .

SON (*grown up*). But Armistice Day brought embarrasing revelaations. We were able to see those from whose loins, as Noah would say, we had actually sprung.

The BOY (*as a boy*) *and* REIGATE *part and move to opposite sides of the stage. On his side, the* BOY *is met by the* MOTHER *and the* FATHER, *come down for the Armistice Day service.* REIGATE *is met by his own* MOTHER, *a short dumpy woman in a hat and rimless spectacles, and his own* FATHER, *a non-descript grey-haired man played by* JAPHET. *Upstage a Union Jack descends. The* HEADMASTER, *to the sound of a bugle playing the Last Post, mounts an open air pulpit wearing on his gown a row of medals.*

HEADMASTER. Let us pray . . .

The parents and the boys form a congregation. MRS REIGATE *closes her eyes in an attitude of devotion. The* FATHER *blows his nose loudly.* REIGATE *stares across at him. The* BOY *looks at his* FATHER *in an agony of embarrassment, and then continues a close, and somewhat surprised study of* REIGATE'S MOTHER.

Oh Lord, inasmuch as we are paraded now on Lower School Field on this, the Armistice Day, November the Eleventh 1936, help us to remember those O.C.'s who fell upon alien soil in the late Great Match. Grant us their spirit, we beseech thee, that we may go 'over the top' to our Common Entrance and our Football Fixtures, armed with the 'cold steel' of Thy Holy Word. Give us, if Thy will be done, the Great Opportunity to shed our Blood for our Country and our Beloved School, and fill us with that feeling of Sportsmanship which led our fathers to fix bayonets and play until the last whistle blew.

THE CONGREGATION (*singing*). 'Lord God of Hosts be with us yet Lest we forget . . . Lest we forget . . .'

REIGATE'S MOTHER *is singing in a rich patriotic contralto. The* FATHER *is singing, and his mouth seems to be moving in a different time from the rest of the congregation. Gradually what he is singing becomes painfully clear over and above the reverberation of the hymn.*

FATHER (*singing*). 'She was as bee-autiful as a butterfly
　　　　　　　　And as proud as a queen
　　　　　　　　Was pretty little Polly Perkins
　　　　　　　　Of Paddington Green'.

Both the FATHER's *song and the hymn come to an end at the same time. The* HEADMASTER *has descended from his pulpit and is saying goodbye, shaking parents' hands. The parents and the* HEADMASTER *go.* REIGATE *and the* BOY *come downstage: chattering idly,* REIGATE's *hands in his pockets: the* BOY *now playing with the yo-yo.*

SON (*grown up*). Our parents, it was obvious, needed a quick coating of romance.

BOY. She didn't look much like a panther.

REIGATE. Who?

BOY. And your mother wasn't exactly a bluebell either . . .

REIGATE. My mother? You've never seen my mother . . .

BOY. Of course I have.

REIGATE. When?

BOY. On Armistice Day . . .

REIGATE. Don't be so simple. That good, honest woman isn't my *real* mother.

BOY (*puzzled*). Noah called her 'Mrs Reigate'. I heard him distinctly.

REIGATE. Noah only knows what's good for him to know. That was no more my mother than you are.

BOY. Who was she then?

REIGATE. Just the dear, good, old soul who promised to look after me.

BOY. When?

REIGATE. When they smuggled me out of Russia, after the revolution. They smuggled me out in a wickerwork trunk. I was ten days and nights on the rack in the carriage of the Siberian Railway. Then we got to Paris . . .

BOY. I thought . . .

REIGATE. They tried to shoot us in Paris. Me and my brother.
But we got away, across the frozen river.

BOY. I thought Siberia was in the other direction.

REIGATE. And escaped to England. This honest chemist and his
wife took care of us. Swear you won't tell anyone?

BOY. All right.

REIGATE. By the blood of my father?

BOY. If you like. I just heard from my parents actually. Something
pretty sensational.

REIGATE. Oh yes?

BOY. I think they're probably . . . getting divorced.

REIGATE (*interested*). Honestly?

BOY. Honestly.

REIGATE. Why? Are they unfaithful?

BOY. Oh, always. And I told you. My mother goes to cocktail
parties . . .

REIGATE (*admiringly*). You'll be having a broken home, then?

BOY (*casual*). Oh yes. I expect I will . . .

The two boys go together. Projection of the garden, trees and flowers.

SON (*grown up, to the audience*). But when I got home, nothing had
changed. My home remained imperturbably intact. And, in the
bracken on the common, Iris had built me a house.

Light on another part of the stage where IRIS *is kneeling, her
skirt up high, her thighs scratched and stained with blackberry
juice. She is arranging a handful of dead wild flowers in a
chipped Coronation mug. The* SON, *as a boy, comes in. He
stands beside her, aloof.*

IRIS. What do you learn at school?

BOY. We learn Latin.

IRIS. What else?

BOY. Greek.

IRIS. Say 'Good morning, what a very nice morning' in Latin.

BOY. I don't know how.

IRIS. All right. In Greek . . .

BOY. I can't.

IRIS. Why not?

BOY. They're not those sort of languages.

IRIS. What's the point of them then?

BOY. They train . . . the mind . . .

IRIS. Do you still whistle?

BOY. Not at school.

IRIS. Why not?

BOY. It's just one of those things you don't do. Like putting your hands in your pockets. You don't whistle, and you don't put your hands in your pockets.

IRIS. Why not?

BOY. You don't. That's all.

IRIS. How's your Mum and Dad?

BOY. Quarrelling.

IRIS. I never see them quarrel.

BOY. It's life . . . They come back from parties, and they quarrel.

IRIS. I shouldn't like that.

BOY. Perhaps they're not my parents, anyway . . .

IRIS. What did you say?

BOY. I said perhaps they're not my parents. Don't ask me to explain.

IRIS. I didn't.

BOY. Well – don't.

IRIS. I shan't.

BOY. It's just possible, they're not my parents. A very honest couple, but not . . .

IRIS. Of course they're your parents. Don't be ignorant.

BOY. I'm not ignorant.

IRIS. What do you know?

BOY. I know the gerund and the gerundive.

IRIS. What are they?

BOY. Something you have. In Latin. And I know the second person plural future passive of rogo.

IRIS. What is it?

BOY. Rogebamini.

IRIS. What's that mean?

BOY. It doesn't mean anything. It's just the future passive of rogo
   – that's all it is . . .

   Pause.

IRIS. This is our house.

BOY (*shrugs his shoulders*). Is it?

IRIS. Shall we be Mothers and Fathers?

BOY. I think I might find that a bit painful, what with the situation
   at home. Anyway, I haven't got time.

IRIS. Haven't you . . .?

BOY. Someone's coming over to see me today.

IRIS. Someone . . .?

BOY. From school. His name's Reigate actually.

IRIS. Don't you want to be Mothers and Fathers . . . (*Gets up
   eagerly.*) Tell you what. I'll let you see . . . (*She pulls up her skirt
   over her head, showing her knickers and a small white stomach.*)

BOY (*backing away from her*). I have to get back. Reigate's
   coming to stay . . .

   Upstage a sofa. The FATHER *is sitting on it.* REIGATE *is on a
   long stool holding tea and cakes. The* MOTHER *crosses to the*
   FATHER *with a cup of tea, kisses him lovingly on the head and
   puts the cup of tea into his hand. The* SON (*as a boy*) *moves into
   the upstage area, collects a cup of tea and a bit of cake and goes
   and sits by* REIGATE *on the stool.*

MOTHER. There's your tea, darling. Be careful now.

   She sits down beside the FATHER *on the sofa.*

REIGATE (*suspiciously to the* BOY). Can't see much sign of divorce
   in this family.

BOY. They're putting on a show – for the visitor.

FATHER. What's going on?

MOTHER. It's the boy talking to Reigate.

FATHER. To who?

MOTHER. To Reigate . . . His friend.

FATHER (*incredulous*). The boy has a friend? (*Sudden bellow.*) Welcome, Reigate! What's Reigate like, eh? Paint me the picture . . .

MOTHER. He's quite small, and . . .

BOY. He's really Russian . . .

FATHER (*impressed*). Russian, eh? Well, that's something of an achievement . . . (*Pause.*) When I was a boy at school I never minded the lessons. I just resented having to work terribly hard at playing. (*Pause.*) They don't roast you at schools now, I suppose? I can't imagine what I'm paying all that money for if they don't roast you from time to time . . .

MOTHER. Do you like the school, Reigate?

REIGATE. It's all right. The headmaster makes us call him Noah.

SON. And his son is Shem.

REIGATE. And we have to call Mr Box and Mr Pearce Ham and Japhet. And we're the animals.

BOY. And Mr Bingo Ollard is Mr Bingo Ollard.

FATHER (*gloomily*). Didn't I warn you? Second rate minds.

> REIGATE *and the* BOY *whisper to each other. Then the* BOY *gets up and goes.*

REIGATE (*to the* MOTHER). We're going to do something to keep you from thinking of your great unhappiness.

MOTHER (*giggles gently*). Our unhappiness . . . Oh . . . Whatever will they think of . . .

FATHER. What're you laughing at?

MOTHER. At Reigate!

FATHER. Who on earth's Reigate?

MOTHER. I told you, dear. The boy's friend.

FATHER. Is this Reigate then, something of a wit?

MOTHER. He does come out with some killing suggestions.

REIGATE (*dignified*). We're going to do a play.

FATHER. What's that?

MOTHER. They're going to put on an entertainment.

The BOY *comes in, dragging an old dressing-up box from which he pulls an old tin hat, a khaki cap, a khaki jacket, a Sam Browne belt, a revolver holster, a water bottle and a bayonet: the* FATHER's *uniform equipment from the 1914 war which he and* REIGATE *proceed to share between them.*

FATHER. I like entertainment. When's it to be?

BOY. This afternoon.

MOTHER. Better hurry. Mr Lean's coming to drive you back to school at four.

FATHER. What is it? Something out of the *Boys' Own?*

BOY. I wrote it.

FATHER. What?

MOTHER. The boy said he wrote it. I'm sure Reigate helped. Didn't you, Reigate?

BOY. He didn't help.

MOTHER. Whatever are you? Two little clowns?

REIGATE. Actually we're two subalterns. Killed on the Somme.

FATHER. Hm. They'll soon be giving us war again. When it comes, remember this. Avoid the temptation to do anything heroic.

REIGATE *goes out of the room, wearing a tin hat and a khaki jacket and the bayonet. The* BOY *is wearing the khaki cap and the Sam Browne.*

Tell me what's going on. Make it vivid.

MOTHER. They've got your barbed wire.

REIGATE *returns pulling a roll of barbed wire which he leaves in the middle of the floor.*

FATHER. My what?

MOTHER. Barbed wire.

FATHER. Put it back, won't you? We don't want the cows in.

MOTHER. Reigate's got your tin hat. And the boy's wearing your old Sam Browne.

FATHER. How killing!

> REIGATE *and the* BOY *take green flashlights from the dressing-up box, turn out the lights in the room and approach each other shining green lights in each other's faces and moaning in a ghostly fashion.*

MOTHER. We can see Reigate's artistic! He's giving a lively performance . . .

REIGATE. Actually we're ghosts.

FATHER. Ghosts eh? What're they doing now.

BOY. We're meeting after the bombardment.

MOTHER. They're meeting after the bombardment, dear.

FATHER. How very killing!

BOY. Bill . . .

REIGATE. Who is it . . .?

BOY. It's me, Bill . . . It's Harry.

REIGATE. Harry! I can't see you, old fellow. (*Coughs.*) It's this damn gas everywhere. Take my hand.

BOY. Where are you?

REIGATE. Out here – by the wire. Listen.

BOY. What?

REIGATE. They've stopped straffing. I say, if ever we get back to the old country –

BOY. What?

REIGATE. I want you to marry Helen.

BOY. You said you'd never let Helen marry a chap who'd funked the top board at Roehampton . . .

REIGATE. Never mind what I said, Harry. I saw you today on the North redoubt; you were in there, batting for England! You shall have my little sister, boy. My hand on it.

BOY. I can't feel your hand, Bill.

REIGATE. I can't see you, Harry.

BOY. I'm cold . . .

REIGATE. I'm afraid we'll never see England again.

BOY. What's the matter with us, Bill?

REIGATE (*beginning to laugh*). We're dead, old fellow. Can't you
understand? We're both of us – dead!

*They are both overcome with laughter and collapse in hoots and
giggles. Their green flashlights go out; and the light is concentrated on the* FATHER *on the sofa while the* MOTHER *supervises
the two boys clearing away the barbed wire, dressing-up box etc.
During the following speech, they all go off with these things,
leaving the* FATHER *alone on the stage.*

FATHER (*laughing*). Dead . . . how killing! (*Serious.*) You know.
I didn't want to be dead. I never wanted that. When I got
married – at Saffron Walden, they were just about to pack me
off to France. Bands. Troop ships. Flowers thrown at you . . .
and dead in a fortnight. I didn't want anything to do with it . . .
And then, the day before we were due to go my old Major drew
me aside and he said 'You've just got married old fellow. No
particular sense in being dead!' He'd found me a post in the
Inland Waterways! That's my advice to you, if they look like
giving us war. Get yourself a job in the Inland Waterways . . .

The light fades on the FATHER *upstage and is concentrated
on* REIGATE *and the* BOY *as they enter upstage in school uniform,
walking side by side. As they start to speak, the* FATHER *gets up,
tapping his way with his stick, leaves the stage.*

REIGATE. Your parents seem to be getting on quite well.
BOY. They pretend – for me.
REIGATE. Your mother didn't seem to drink very much either.
BOY. Not till the evenings.

Light increases upstage where JAPHET *enters with a portable
gramophone which he puts down on a table and puts on a record.*

REIGATE. That was good advice your father gave us – about the
Inland Waterways . . .
BOY. Yes.
REIGATE. You know? I'll tell you something about your father . . .

BOY. What?

REIGATE. He can't see . . . He's blind, isn't he?

SON (*grown up, to the audience*). It was a question our family never asked. Naturally I didn't answer it.

> *Pause. The* SON (*as a boy*) *says nothing.* JAPHET's *record starts to play 'Smoke gets in your eyes'. The* BOY *turns sharply away from* REIGATE *and moves towards* JAPHET. JAPHET *holds up his arms and he and the* BOY *silently start to dance together to 'Smoke gets in your eyes'.* REIGATE *looks after the son, shrugs his shoulders then crosses the stage and goes.*

JAPHET. Slow, quick, slow. Slow, quick, slow. Chassis! No – chassis! Look! (*They dance a few more bars together, awkwardly, at arm's length.*) How're you going to get through life if you can't do the slow foxtrot . . .? That's the trouble with education. It never teaches you anything worth knowing. Half the boys here've got no idea of tying their ties, let alone tango . . . Sorry you're leaving . . .?

BOY. Not altogether . . .

> *The music stops.* JAPHET *takes off the record, studies it, embarrassed.*

JAPHET. I'm leaving too. Perhaps you heard . . .?

BOY. Yes, sir, I know. Lydia left yesterday. We had to make our own beds this morning.

JAPHET. Lydia's left. I've resigned. So has the poor old King.

BOY. Him as well . . .?

JAPHET. He broadcast this afternoon. We heard it on Noah's radiogram. The King has given up everything for love. I told you we had a lot in common . . .

> *Pause.*

Take my advice. Don't give up everything for love . . .

BOY. No, sir.

JAPHET. It's just not on – that's all. Just simply not on . . .

BOY. You coming to Noah's talk, sir? It's for all of us leavers.

JAPHET. The one where he tells you the facts of life . . .?

BOY. I think that's the one.

JAPHET. No. I shall stay away. I've heard quite enough about *them* to be going on with . . .

> The HEADMASTER *appears downstage, wearing a tweed jacket with leather patches and smoking a pipe.* REIGATE *comes in and sits on the floor gazing up at him respectfully.* JAPHET, *upstage, packs up his gramophone and goes. The* BOY *moves upstage.*

HEADMASTER. You are the leavers! In a month or two you will go on to Great Public Schools, away from this warm cosy little establishment. (*The* BOY *arrives and stands and knocks.*) Come in. You're disturbing everybody. Shut the door, boy. Most terrible draught. (*The* BOY *moves in and sits down next to* REIGATE.) Ah now . . . Before I forget, Mrs Noah and I will be pleased to see you all to tea on Sunday. A trifling matter of anchovy paste sandwiches! Do you hear that, eh Reigate? All come with clean finger nails, no boy to put butter on his hair.

REIGATE. Please, sir?

HEADMASTER. Yes, Reigate.

REIGATE. Why aren't we to put butter on our hair?

HEADMASTER. Ah! Good question. I'm glad you asked me that! We had that trouble with the native regiments. They licked down their hair with butter. It went rancid in the hot weather. Unpleasant odour on parade. There's no law against a drop of water on the comb. Now . . . What was I going to tell you? Ah! I was warning you about dreams. You'll have them. Oh, certainly you'll have them. And in the morning you may feel like saying to yourselves, 'You rotter! To have a dream like that!' Well, you can't help it. That's all. You simply can't help them. Not dreams. If you're awake of course, you can do something about it. You can change into a pair of shorts and go for a run across country. Or you can get into a bath, and turn on the cold tap. You can quite easily do that. Your housemaster will understand. He'll understand if you should've been up to a French lesson, or Matins or some such thing. Simply say, Sir, I had to have a bath, or a run, or whatever it is. Just say to Mr Raffles, or Humphrey Stiggler, or Percy Parr, just say, Mr Parr, or Mr Raffles, dependant on which school you're at of course, this is what I felt the need to do. He'll understand perfectly. Another thing! Simply this. When sleeping always lie on the right side. Not on the face, for obvious reasons. Not on the back. Brings on dreams. Not on the left side. Stops the heart. Just the right side . . . all the time. Now then, to the most serious problems you're likely to run up against. Friends. You may find that some boy from another class, or a house even, comes up to you and says 'Let's be friends' or even offers you a slice of cake. That's a very simple one, a perfectly simple one to deal with. Just say loudly 'I'm going straight to tell the housemaster'. Straight away. No hesitation about it. Remember, the only real drawback to our Great Public School system is unsolicited cake – Have you got that very clear? Go straight and tell the Housemaster.

> BOY *and* REIGATE *get up, stretch, and wander off.* REIGATE *playing with the yo-yo which he gets out of his pocket.*

REIGATE. Do you have dreams?

BOY. Not very much . . .

REIGATE. I once dreamt about fish.

BOY. What?

REIGATE. All that fish. You know the fish we had on Sunday nights. That we put down the loo. I dreamt it came swimming back at us. I dreamt it all swam back in shoals, and invaded the school.

BOY. Did you feel bad? About dreaming that, I mean.

REIGATE. I suppose so.

BOY. That must've been what he meant.

> *They go. Upstage lit, the* FATHER *and* MOTHER *are sitting on two garden chairs, beside a tea trolley. An empty chair beside them. Downstage the* SON *(grown up) speaks to the audience, he*

*is putting on a school blazer and knitting a silk scarf round his
neck.*

SON (*grown up*). It wasn't until later that I realized the headmaster
had been trying to advise us on a subject my father often
brought up unexpectedly, in the middle of tea.

> *The* SON (*as a boy*) *enters upstage, sits in the empty chair beside
> his* FATHER *and* MOTHER, *takes a biscuit, lounges, chewing it as
> the* MOTHER *pours tea. Pause, before the* FATHER *speaks.*

FATHER. Sex! It's been greatly over-rated by the poets . . .

MOTHER. Would you like your biscuit now, dear? (*She puts a
biscuit beside him on a plate.*)

FATHER. I never had many mistresses with thighs like white
marble. Is the tea pot exhausted?

MOTHER. I'm putting some more hot water in now.

> *The* MOTHER *continues pouring tea. The meal goes on.*

SON (*grown up, to the audience*). What did he mean? That he'd
had many mistresses without especially marmoreal thighs – or
few mistresses of any sort?

FATHER (*suddenly*). 'Change in a trice
The lilies and languors of virtue
For the roses and raptures of vice!'
Where's my bloody biscuit . . .?

MOTHER. I put it beside you, dear.

FATHER. 'From their lips have thy lips taken fever?
Is the breath of them hot in thy hair . . .?'

SON (*grown up, to the audience*). What did he know of the sharp
uncertainties of love?

> *The* SON (*grown up*) *turns and moves upstage. He taps the* BOY
> *on the shoulder and motions him to move. The* BOY *gets up
> reluctantly and leaves the stage, chewing his biscuit. The* SON
> (*grown up*) *takes his chair and sits, the* MOTHER *hands him a
> cup of tea.*

c

FATHER (*suddenly laughing*). 'Is the breath of them hot in thy hair?' How perfectly revolting it sounds! Sex is pretty uphill work, if you want my opinion.

SON. I don't agree.

FATHER. What?

SON. I don't happen to agree.

FATHER. Who's that?

MOTHER. It's the boy. (*She looks at him, gives a small laugh.*) Whatever have you got on?

FATHER. The boy's been very quiet lately.

MOTHER. He's wearing my old scarf from Liberties. Tied as a cravat.

FATHER. A cravat eh? How killing! (*Pause.*) Is that what it is? Do you have your own thoughts?

SON. I don't think sex has been overrated exactly.

FATHER. I'll tell you a story. A lover, a wife and an angry husband . . .

MOTHER (*calm*). Not that one, dear. (*To the* SON.) You'll have some tea?

FATHER. Whyever not?

MOTHER. It's not very suitable. (*To the* SON, *vaguely*) Do you like sugar? I always forget.

SON. No thanks.

FATHER. The husband returns and discovers all! He summons the lover into the dining room. The wife waits, trembling, terrified, for the sounds of fighting, the smashing of crockery. Silence. She tiptoes down the stairs. There's the husband and the lover side by side at the table, perfectly contented, drinking light ale. Suddenly she bursts out at both of them – 'You ungrateful brutes!' They both listen as the door slams after her. They open another bottle of light ale. 'Ungrateful brutes!' That was the expression she used!

Pause. The SON *looks at him.*

SON. Did that really happen?

FATHER. What?

SON. Did that ever really happen?

Pause.

FATHER. Sex! The whole business has been over-estimated by the poets.

The SON *looks at his watch, gets up, kisses his* MOTHER *and moves downstage. He takes a cigarette case out of his inside blazer pocket and lights a cigarette with careless expertise. He moves to a downstage corner where, separately and pinkly lit, two women enter smoking through holders. They are* MISS COX, *small and fluffy, nursing a poodle, and* MISS BAKER, *in trousers and a beret. Furniture set in their area includes a drawing by Cocteau of a sailor, and a white macaw in a cage. Somewhere a portable radio is softly playing 'La Vie en Rose' as* MISS BAKER *hands pink drinks to* MISS COX *and the* SON.

Upstage the FATHER *and the* MOTHER *continue to talk.*

FATHER. Where's the boy?

MOTHER. Gone out. He's paying a call.

FATHER (*incredulous*). Gone out – as a visitor?

MOTHER. Yes. To tea. With Miss Baker and Miss Cox.

FATHER. Who are they?

MOTHER. They run the new book shop. By the station. Apparently he went in to buy a book and they asked him round to tea – as a visitor. I expect that's the notion behind his extraordinary cravat.

FATHER. Not bringing them back here, is he?

MOTHER. He didn't say so.

FATHER. If he does, I shall lie doggo! I shall go to earth, in the West Copse. I shall hide myself . . . I promise you . . .

MOTHER. No, he didn't say he was bringing them back here . . .

FATHER. Well, I shall disappear without a trace if he does.

He feels for his stick, struggles to his feet. The MOTHER *stands up and takes his arm.*

Doesn't he know? We dread visitors. (*Pause.*) Poor boy, to have to go out. He'll miss the evening foray after earwigs.

The MOTHER *and the* FATHER *walk off together.*

MISS COX. I could've kissed you when you came in to our shop.

SON. Could you really?

MISS BAKER. And actually bought a book!

MISS COX. Most people come in for pamphlets. A hundred things to do with dried egg – published by the Ministry of Food . . .

The radio stops playing 'La Vie en Rose'. A BBC ANNOUNCER *speaks cheerily.*

ANNOUNCER'S VOICE. 'What do I do if I come across German or Italian broadcasts when tuning my wireless? I say to myself: "Now this blighter wants me to listen to him. Am I going to do what this blighter wants?"'

MISS BAKER (*switches the radio off*). We'll have to give up that shop.

SON. Why will you?

MISS COX. Bill's going to be called up.

SON. Who's Bill?

MISS BAKER I'm Bill. (*She picks up a bit of bread and butter and waves it at* MISS COX.) She's Daphne . . . (*She goes to the macaw's cage, prods a piece of bread and butter through the cage bars.*) . . . This bloody bird gets half my butter ration . . .

MISS COX. They're putting Bill on the land . . .

MISS BAKER. I'll probably ruin the crops.

MISS COX. I'll send you off in the morning darling . . . with a meat pie and a little bottle of cold tea.

MISS BAKER. Thank you very much!

MISS COX. It's the war, Bill! We all have to make sacrifices. (*To* SON.) Bill doesn't much care for this war. We were more keen on the war in Spain.

MISS BAKER. And in the evenings, I suppose you'll wash me down in front of the fire. (*To the macaw.*) Eat up, Miss Garbo!

MISS COX. Nonsense. They're not sending you down the mines!
(*To the* SON.) All our friends were awfully keen on the war in
Spain; Stephen Spender and all that jolly collection . . . I expect
you'll go into the Fire Service . . .?

SON. Why?

MISS COX. All our friends go into the Fire Service.

MISS BAKER. They get a lot of time for writing, waiting about
between fires . . .

SON. My father says I should avoid the temptation to do anything
heroic . . .

Change of light, projection of a darker garden upstage. The
MOTHER *comes in, leading the* FATHER, *carrying his camp stool
and a bucket. She sits him down in front of a plant with inverted
flower pots on a stick around it. Then she leaves him. He begins
to feel for the pots and empty them in the bucket.*

MISS COX. We've never actually met your father . . .

MISS BAKER. We looked over the gate one evening and shouted –
but he was busy in the garden doing something.

SON. Probably the earwigs.

MISS BAKER. What?

SON. He drowns the earwigs every night.

MISS COX. How most extraordinary . . .

She gets up and starts putting things back on the tea tray.

The Fire Service! That's where you'll end up. It gives everyone
far more time to write.

MISS BAKER. Is that what you're going to be then – a writer?

Pause. Change of light. The light fades on MISS COX *and*
MISS BAKER'S *part of the stage, and increases on the* FATHER
as the SON *leaves the two ladies, and walks across to join the*
FATHER. *On his way he collects a camp stool and puts it up and
sits beside the* FATHER. *He starts to help him with the earwig
traps, taking off the inverted flower pots and emptying the ear-*

*wigs that have gone in there for warmth and shelter, into the
bucket of water to drown miserably.* MISS BAKER *and* MISS
COX *go.*

FATHER. Is that you?

SON. Yes, it's me.

FATHER. What're you doing?

SON. Helping you.

FATHER. Consider the persistence of the earwig! Each afternoon,
it feasts on the dahlia blooms. Each night it crawls into our
flower pots to sleep. Each morning, we empty the flower pots
and drown the earwig . . . but still they come! Nature's remorse-
less.

SON. I may be a writer . . .

FATHER. If we did this for one million years all over the world,
could we make some small dent in the pattern of evolution?
Would we produce an earwig that could swim? (*Pause.*) You'd
be better off in the law . . .

SON. I'd like to write . . .

FATHER. You'll have plenty of spare time! My first five years in
Chambers, I did nothing but *The Times* crossword puzzle.
Besides which, if you were only a writer, who would you rub
shoulders with? (*With contempt.*) Other writers? You'll be far
better off in the law.

SON. I don't know . . .

FATHER. No brilliance is needed in the law. Nothing but common
sense, and relatively clean finger nails. Another thing, if you
were a writer, think of your poor, unfortunate wife . . .

SON. What?

FATHER. She'd have you at home every day! In carpet slippers . . .
Drinking tea and stumped for words! You'd be far better off
down the tube each morning, and off to the Law Courts . . .
How many have we bagged today?

SON (*looking down into the bucket*). About a hundred.

FATHER. A moderate bag, I'd say. Merely moderate. You know,

the law of husband and wife might seem idiotic at first sight. But when you get to know it, you'll find it can exercise a vague medieval charm. Learn a little law, won't you? Just to please me . . .

The MOTHER *enters. She goes up to the* FATHER, *touches him.*

MOTHER. Your bath's ready.

FATHER. What?

MOTHER. I said your bath water's nice and hot.

He gets up, takes her arm. She starts to lead him off the stage.

I suppose there isn't an easier way of getting rid of earwigs?

FATHER. An easier way! Sometimes I wonder if women understand anything.

They go. The SON *stands, then moves down towards the audience. The light changes and the garden fades on the back-cloth, to be replaced by a pattern of Gothic arches. The* SON *speaks to the audience, downstage right.*

SON. It was my father's way to offer the law to me – the great stone column of authority which has been dragged by an adulterous, careless, negligent and half criminal humanity down the ages – as if it were a small mechanical toy which might occupy half an hour on a rainy afternoon.

Upstage a Judge's chair with a coat of arms, a witness box. A JUDGE *enters, and takes his place: from offstage left, the sound of footsteps on a stone passage and the tapping of a stick. Then the* FATHER *and* MOTHER *enter downstage left. The* FATHER *is now wearing a black jacket and a winged collar and bow tie. The* MOTHER *stations the* FATHER *by one of the cubes on which a mirror is hanging. She goes out and returns with his wig, gown and white bands to take the place of his tie, and helps him to change. The opposing barrister,* MR BOUSTEAD, *robed, but carrying his wig, comes and starts to comb his hair in front of the mirror.*

SON (*to the audience*). He never used a white stick – but his clouded malacca was heard daily, tapping the cold stone corridors of the Law Courts. He had no use for dogs, therapy, training, nor did he adapt himself to his condition. He simply pretended that nothing had happened. (*The* SON *goes.*)

BOUSTEAD. Good morning.

FATHER. Who's that?

MOTHER. It's Mr Boustead, dear . . . He's for the husband.

FATHER. Agin me, Bulstrode. Are you agin me?

BOUSTEAD. Boustead.

FATHER. Excuse me. Boustead of course. Where are you?

BOUSTEAD. Here, I'm here . . .

FATHER. I have studied your case pretty closely and I have a suggestion to make which you might find helpful.

BOUSTEAD. Really?

FATHER. What I was suggesting, entirely for your assistance of course – is that you might like – my dear boy – to throw in your hand . . . Now, is that a help to you . . .?

BOUSTEAD. Certainly not! I'd say we have some pretty valuable evidence . . .

> *Light change. In the witness box appears* MR THONG, *a private detective of a crafty appearance, wearing a brown suit and a cycling club badge on his lapel.* BOUSTEAD *moves to upstage right, stands questioning him. The* MOTHER *leads the* FATHER *to his seat left and sits behind him.*

BOUSTEAD. Now from the vantage point which you have described, Mr Thong, will you tell my Lord and the Jury exactly what you saw?

> *The* FATHER *turns and speaks in a loud stage whisper to the* MOTHER.

FATHER. Throat spray!

> *The* MOTHER *puts a small throat spray into the* FATHER'S *hand.* THONG *consults his notebook.*

BOUSTEAD. Yes, Mr Thong, in your own words.

FATHER (*loud whisper*). Thanks.

THONG (*monotonously, reading his notebook*). From my point of vantage, I was quite clearly able to see inside the kitchen window . . .

BOUSTEAD. Yes?

THONG. And –

> The FATHER *opens his mouth and starts, very loudly, to spray his throat.*

JUDGE. Speak up, Mr Thong, I can't hear you.

THONG. My Lord. I was able to distinguish clearly the Respondent . . .

JUDGE (*writing carefully*). Yes. . .

THONG. In the act of . . . (*His mumble is again drowned by the* FATHER's *work with the throat spray.*) . . . with a man distinguishable only by a small moustache . . . I now recognize him as the Co-Respondent, Dacres.

BOUSTEAD. In the act of what, Mr Thong?

THONG. The act of . . . (*The* FATHER *works the throat spray very loudly.*

BOUSTEAD. If my learned friend would allow us to hear the evidence . . .

FATHER (*puts down the throat spray and whispers deafeningly to* BOUSTEAD). I'm so sorry. My dear boy, if *this* is the valuable evidence you told me about, I shall be quiet – as the tomb . . .!

BOUSTEAD (*firmly*). Mr Thong.

FATHER (*half rising to address the* JUDGE). By all means, my Lord. Let us hear this *valuable* evidence.

JUDGE. Very well.

THONG. I distinctly saw them . . .

JUDGE. Distinctly saw them what?

THONG. Kissing and cuddling, my Lord.

BOUSTEAD. And then . . .

THONG. The light was extinguished . . .

BOUSTEAD. Where?

THONG. In the kitchen.

BOUSTEAD. And a further light appeared?

THONG. In the bedroom.

JUDGE. For a moment?

THONG. Merely momentarily, my Lord.

BOUSTEAD. So . . .

THONG. The house was shrouded in darkness. And the Co-Respondent, this is the point that struck us, had not emerged.

BOUSTEAD. And you kept up observation until . . .

THONG. Approximately, dawn.

BOUSTEAD (*very satisfied, as he sits down*). Thank you, Mr Thong.

The FATHER *rises, clattering. Folds his hands on his stomach, gazes sightlessly at* MR THONG *and then allows a long pause during which* MR THONG *stirs uncomfortably. Then he starts quietly, slowly working himself up into a climax.*

FATHER. Mr Thong, what price did you put on this valuable evidence?

THONG. I don't know what you mean . . .

FATHER. You have been paid, haven't you, to give it?

THONG. I'm a private enquiry agent . . .

FATHER. A professional witness?

THONG. Charging the usual fee.

FATHER. Thirty pieces of silver?

BOUSTEAD (*rises, indignant*). My Lord, I object. This is outrageous.

JUDGE. Perhaps that was not entirely relevant. (BOUSTEAD *subsides.*)

FATHER. Then let me ask you something which is very relevant. Which goes straight to the secret heart of this wretched little conspiracy. Where was this lady's husband during your observations?

THONG. Captain Waring?

FATHER. Yes. Captain Waring.

THONG. He had accompanied me . . .

FATHER. Why?

THONG. For the purpose of . . .

FATHER. For the purpose of what . . .?

THONG. Identification . . .

FATHER. And how long did he remain with you?

THONG. As long as observation continued . . .

FATHER. Till dawn . . .?

THONG. Until approximately 5.30 a.m.

FATHER. And did he not storm the house? Did he not beat upon the door? Did he not seize his wife's paramour by the throat and hurl him into the gutter?

THONG. According to my notebook. No.

FATHER. And according to your notebook, was he enjoying himself?

BOUSTEAD (*driven beyond endurance, rises to protest*). Really . . .!

FATHER. Please, Mr Bulstrode! I've sat here for three days! Like patience on a monument! Whilst a series of spiteful, mean, petty, trumped-up sickening and small-minded charges are tediously paraded against the unfortunate woman I represent. And now, when I rise to cross-examine . . . *I will not be interrupted!*

JUDGE. Gentlemen! Please, gentlemen. (*To* FATHER.) What was your question?

FATHER. I've forgotten it. My learned friend's interruption has had the effect he no doubt intended and I have forgotten my question!

BOUSTEAD. This is quite intolerable . . .

FATHER. Ah . . . Now I've remembered it again. Did he enjoy the night, Thong, in this field . . . from which he was magically able to overlook his own kitchen . . .?

THONG. This plot of waste ground . . .

FATHER. Up a tree, was he?

THONG. What?

FATHER. Was he perched upon a tree?

THONG. We had stepped up, into the lower branches.

FATHER. Was it the naked eye?

THONG. Pardon?

FATHER. Was he viewing this distressing scene by aid of the naked eye?

THONG. Captain Waring had brought a pair of field glasses.

FATHER. His racing glasses . . .?

THONG. I . . .

JUDGE. Speak up, Mr Thong.

THONG. I imagine he used them for racing, my Lord.

FATHER. You see Captain Waring has given evidence in this Court.

BOUSTEAD (*ironic*). On the subject of his racing glasses?

FATHER (*his voice filled with passion*). No, Mr Bulstrode. On the subject of love. He has told us that he was deeply, sincerely in love with his wife.

THONG. I don't know anything about that.

FATHER. Exactly, Mr Thong! You are hardly an expert witness, are you, on the subject of love?

Light change. MR THONG *leaves the witness box.* BOUSTEAD *leaves also. The* FATHER *is standing as if addressing the Jury.*

May it please you, my Lord, Members of the Jury. Love has driven men and women in the course of history to curious extremes. Love tempted Leander to plunge in and swim the raging Hellespont. It led Juliet to feign death and Ophelia to madness. No doubt it complicated the serenity of the Garden of Eden and started the Trojan War: but surely there is no more curious example of the mysterious effects of the passion than the spectacle of Captain Waring of the Royal Engineers, roosted in a tree, complacently viewing the seduction of his beloved through a pair of strong racing binoculars . . .

The light fades altogether on the back of the upstage areas. The FATHER's *voice comes out of the shadows.*

Is not the whole story, Members of the Jury, an improbable and impertinent tissue of falsehood . . .?

The SON *is lit downstage as in the upstage darkness, the* JUDGE, *the* FATHER, *and the* MOTHER *go and the Courtroom furniture is moved away.*

SON (*to the audience*). He sent words out into the darkness, like soldiers sent off to battle, and was never short of reinforcements. In the Law Courts he gave his public performance. At home he returned to his private ritual, the potting shed, the crossword puzzle and, when I was at home, the afternoon walk.

Projection of trees as the upstage area becomes slowly lighter.

The woods were dark and full of flies. We picked bracken leaves to swat them, and when I was a child he told me we carried cutlasses to hack our way through the jungle. I used to shut my eyes at dead rats, or magpies gibbeted on the trees: sights his blindness spared him. He walked with his hand on my arm. A small hand, with loose brown skin. From time to time, I had an urge to pull away from him, to run into the trees and hide . . . to leave him alone, lost in perpetual darkness. But then his hand would tighten on my sleeve; he was very persistent . . .

The SON *walks behind a cube and emerges with the* FATHER *who is wearing a tweed jacket and his straw hat and is holding the* SON's *arm tightly as they walk round the stage, slowly towards a raised platform upstage . . .*

FATHER. I've had a good deal of fun . . . out of the law.

SON. Have you ever been to the South of France?

FATHER. Once or twice. It's all right, except for the dreadful greasy food they can't stop talking about.

SON. Bill and Daphne say the worst of the War is that they can't get to the South of France.

FATHER. Who're they?

SON. Two ladies from the book shop.

FATHER. Where you had to go, as a visitor?

SON. That's right.

FATHER. My heart bled for you on that occasion.

SON. Daphne's Miss Cox.

FATHER. And Bill . . .?

SON. . . . Bill's Miss Baker.

FATHER. Damned rum!

SON. Before the War they practically lived in Cannes. They met Cocteau . . .

FATHER. Who?

SON. He smoked opium. Have you ever smoked opium?

FATHER. Certainly not! Gives you constipation. Dreadful binding effect. Ever seen those pictures of the wretched poet Coleridge? Green around the gills. And a stranger to the lavatory. Avoid opium.

SON. They may find me a war job.

FATHER. Who?

SON. Miss Baker and Miss Cox.

FATHER. Why, is 'Bill' on the General Staff?

SON. They have a friend who makes propaganda films for the government. He needs an assistant.

FATHER. You're thinking of entering the film world?

SON. Just . . . for the duration.

FATHER. Well! At least there's nothing heroic about it.

SON. No.

FATHER. Rum sort of world, isn't it – the film world?

SON. I expect so.

FATHER. Don't they wear their caps *back to front* in the film world?

SON. You're thinking of the silent days.

FATHER. Am I? Perhaps I am. Your mother and I went to a silent film once. In Glastonbury.

SON. Did you?

FATHER. We were staying there in an hotel. Damn dull. Nothing to do in the evenings. So we sallied forth, to see this silent film.

The point was, I invariably dressed for dinner, when in Glastonbury. Follow?

SON. I follow.

FATHER. And when your mother and I entered this picture palace – in evening dress – the whole audience burst into spontaneous applause! I believe they took us for part of the entertainment! . . . Rum kind of world I must say. Where are we?

SON. At the bottom of Stonor hill.

FATHER. I'll rest for a moment. Then we'll go up to the top.

The SON *moves him to the right of the platform and sits him down.*

SON. Will we?

FATHER. Of course we will! You can see the three counties from the top of Stonor Hill. Don't you want to see three counties . . .?

SON. All right.

FATHER. See everything. Everything in Nature . . . That's the instinct of the May beetle. Twenty-four hours to live, so spend it . . . looking around.

SON. We've got more time . . .

FATHER. Don't you believe it! It's short . . . but enjoyable! You know what? If they ever say to you – 'your old Father, he couldn't have enjoyed life much. Overdrawn at the Bank and bad-tempered and people didn't often visit him . . .' 'Nonsense' you can say. 'He enjoyed every minute of it . . .'

SON. Do you want to go on now?

FATHER. When you consider the embryo of the liver fluke, born in sheeps' droppings, searching the world for a shell to bore into for the sake of living in a snail until it becomes tadpole-like and leaves its host – and then gets swallowed up by a sheep again! When you consider that – complicated persistence, well, of course, I've clung on for sixty five years. It's the instinct – that's all. The irresistible instinct! All right. We'll go up . . . Watch carefully and you'll see three counties . . .

He puts out his hand, the SON *pulls him up. They walk off behind a cube. Light change. The projection of trees changes to blue sky*

and small clouds. On the platform, MISS COX *and* MISS
BAKER *are sunbathing : wearing bathing suits, lying on a rug,
their arms around each other. They are kissing as the* FATHER
and SON *re-appear breathless after their climb. The* SON *says
nothing.* MISS BAKER *puts a hand over* MISS COX's *mouth.*

What can you see?

SON. Three counties . . .

FATHER. Be my eyes then. Paint me the picture . . .

SON (*pause*). We can just see three counties. Stretched out. That's
all we can see.

FATHER. A fine prospect?

SON. Yes. A fine prospect.

FATHER. We've bagged a good many sights today! What've we
seen?

SON. We saw a hare. Oh, and that butterfly.

FATHER. Danaius Chrysippus! The one that flaunts a large type
of powder puff. You described it to me. You painted me the
picture.

SON. Shall we go home now?

FATHER. We saw a lot today.

As the SON *moves back towards the door the* FATHER *moves
with him.*

We saw a good deal – of the monstrous persistence of Nature . . .

The FATHER *and the* SON *move away.* MISS BAKER *takes her
hand off* MISS COX's *mouth releasing a cascade of giggles as the
light fades.*

ACT TWO

Light downstage. Noise of carpentry, shouting, singing and cursing. A movie camera on a tripod is set somewhere downstage. Film technicians, a SPARKS *trundling a 2K and a* CHIPPY *with a trestle and a bit of wood, enter. The* CHIPPY *starts to saw noisily. The* DIRECTOR, *wearing a sheepskin flying jacket, fur boots and a woollen hat, comes in smoking a Wills Whiff and looks into the camera. The stage management of the play should come on the stage in this scene and become the film technicians, cameramen etc. Projection on the backcloth suggests a cloudy sky, a radar installation and observation post 'somewhere in England during the War'.*

SPARKS (*singing loudly*).
> 'Oh Salome, Salome
> That's my girl, Salome.
> Standing there with her arse all bare . . .'

The SON *enters. He is carrying a glossy magazine called* Kinema Arts *and wearing dark glasses. He looks round, lost.* DORIS *enters. She's the Unit Manager. A tough, very competent, deep voiced woman also wearing a sheepskin flying jacket, flying boots and a G.I.'s cap on her orange hair. She also has a cigarette drooping from pillarbox red lips, and is carrying a clip board with the script, schedule etc. on it. She approaches the* SON *with a military swagger.*

DORIS (*yells*). Let's have some quiet please! (*The noise stops. To* SON.) You the new assistant . . .?
SON (*nervous*). Yes?
SPARKS (*singing quietly*).
> 'Every little wrinkle made the boys all stare . . .'

D

DORIS (*full throated roar*). Great Scott, Sparks! I can't hear this boy.

SPARKS. Sorry, Doris.

He stops singing.

DORIS. Know your job, do you . . .?

SON. I'm new to movies . . .

DORIS. Great Scott! You don't have to know anything about movies. You're here to fetch the subsistence . . .

SON. The what?

DORIS. Tea breaks. Coffee breaks. After lunch special refreshment and in lieu of breakfast breaks. The Sparks have tea and ham and lettuce rolls, known to them as smiggett sandwiches. The Chippies take coffee and cakes with coconut icing. The director needs Horlicks, liver pâté sandwiches and Wills Whiffs. Keep your mouth shut except to call in a firm and authoritative manner for 'Quiet' when we shoot. Any questions?

SON. Yes.

DORIS. What?

SON. Where do I get liver pâté sandwiches?

DORIS. Use your bloody imagination! That's what you came into the film business for . . .

DIRECTOR (*calling her from the camera*). Doris!

DORIS. Coming, Humphrey. (*To the* SON.) Remember, next tea break in ten minutes. (*She goes to chatter to the* DIRECTOR.)

SPARKS *comes up to the puzzled looking* SON. *Talks at great speed.*

SPARKS. You looking for something?

SON. Well, yes.

SPARKS. Don't worry. Maybe you left it in the Officers' Mess. You know we've got two ATS in the next scene?

SON. I didn't know.

SPARKS. There's two sorts of ATS let me tell you. Cocked ATS and felt ATS. Had it in last night, did you?

SON. What did you say?

SPARKS. Seen the King last night?

SON. No. (*Innocent*.) Was he here?

SPARKS. Was he here! . . . That's a good one. Who did you say you was out with?

Upstage two ATS girls apppear in uniform. One scans the sky with binoculars. The other starts to pour tea. The camera is focused on them. A STAGE MANAGER *holds a microphone on the end of a long bamboo pole near to them.*

SON. Actually . . . No one.

SPARKS. Didn't spend out on her, I hope? Never spend out till you get lucky . . . Then you can buy her a packet of small smokes.

DIRECTOR. All right, we'll try a rehearsal.

SPARKS. What did you say you was looking for?

SON. A liver pâté sandwich.

SPARKS. A liver pâté . . . You're a caution! That's what you are.

DORIS. Rehearsal!

The ATS GIRLS *start to speak.* SPARKS *returns to his light which is switched on them. The* SON *wanders off disconsolately. Other members of the Unit start a game of pontoon somewhere.*

FIRST ATS GIRL. Gerry a bit naughty tonight, Hilda.

SECOND ATS GIRL. Yes. (*She offers the other a mug of tea.*) Tea, luv?

FIRST ATS GIRL (*lowers her binoculars*). Ta, luv.

SECOND ATS GIRL. Sugars, do you?

FIRST ATS GIRL. Ta.

SECOND ATS GIRL. One or two sugars?

FIRST ATS GIRL. Two, ta. (*Pause*). Ta.

Pause.

SECOND ATS GIRL. You know, I've been thinking lately.

FIRST ATS GIRL. Have you, luv?

The SON *comes back with a tray, starts handing tea and sandwiches round the Unit.*

SECOND ATS GIRL. Oh yes, Hilda, I've been thinking.

FIRST ATS GIRL. What about, luv?

SECOND ATS GIRL. You know what I reckon this war's all about?

Long pause.

FIRST ATS GIRL. No.

SECOND ATS GIRL. Just our freedom. To talk to each other.

FIRST ATS GIRL. You want sugar, luv?

DIRECTOR. That was marvellous. Tremendously real. My God, you couldn't do that with actors! All right, Doris. I'm going for a take.

DORIS. Assistant! Get a bit of silence will you?

SON (*moving away from the tea tray*). Sorry Doris . . .

DORIS. Yell 'Quiet' for God's sake.

SON (*moves to the centre of the stage, clears his throat and says very nervously*). Quiet, please!

The noise of the Unit continues.

Can we have a little quiet now, please?

From this moment, the noise intensifies, the CHIPPY *saws at his bit of wood.* SPARKS *sings 'Oh, Salome' and hammers at his 2K. The pontoon game erupts into a loud argument and the two ATS girls start to dance together, humming 'The White Cliffs of Dover'. The light concentrates on the* SON, *fading on the rest of the stage as he becomes more and more panic-stricken.*

SON. We'd appreciate a bit of quiet now, thank you!

Noise.

All quiet now! We're going to try a take.

Noise.

Ladies and gentlemen, will you please give us a little QUIET!

Noise.

QUIET now PLEASE!

There is increased noise. He now sounds hysterical as he yells.

SHUT UP, YOU BASTARDS!

Total silence. Everyone except the SON *quietly leaves the stage, taking with them the paraphernalia of the film unit. The* SON *is left alone. Light change. Upstage a dark girl,* ELIZABETH, *comes in with a chair and sits down to a portable typewriter, puts in paper, lights a cigarette and starts at it. She is dark, beautiful, wearing tight corduroy trousers and a fisherman's sweater.*

SON (*moving towards her*). Is this the writer's department?

The typing continues.

They said I'm not cut out by nature to be an Assistant Director. When I called for 'Quiet' all the electricians went on strike.

The typing continues.

They said with me as an Assistant Director the War'd be over before they finished the movie.

She stops typing, looks up at him and smiles for the first time. Encouraged he goes and looks at what she is typing.

What's the script?

ELIZABETH. It's something Humphrey wants to do. (*She pulls a face.*) There's a character in it called the 'Common Man'. He keeps saying 'Look here, matey, what *is* the World Health Organization?'.

SON. Sounds ghastly.

ELIZABETH (*smiles*). Yes, it is rather.

SON (*sits on the edge of her table*). What on earth do you want to write that for?

ELIZABETH I suppose . . . the school fees.

SON. You studying something?

ELIZABETH (*laughing*). No, you fool. My kids . . . Peter's only got his Captain's pay and . . .

SON. Peter?

ELIZABETH. My husband.

SON (*getting up and moving away from her*). He's abroad?

ELIZABETH. Uxbridge. In Army education.

SON. My father says . . . in time of War you should avoid the temptation to do anything heroic.

ELIZABETH. How odd.

SON. What?

ELIZABETH. What an odd thing for him to say.

SON. You know, after today I think I'll abandon the film business and take up the Law.

Pause. She doesn't react.

My father's a Lawyer.

ELIZABETH. Do you always copy your father?

SON. Good God no!

ELIZABETH. Really? (*She pushes her hair back and looks at him, her long legs stretched out, her hands in her trouser pockets.*) You look the type to agree with Dad.

SON (*looking at her*). There's one thing he says I don't agree with at all.

ELIZABETH. What's that?

SON moves to her table. Takes one of her cigarettes, lights it, blows out smoke, doing his best to be elegant and casual.

SON. He says that sex has been greatly overrated. By the poets . . .

Upstage, light fades. Downstage the FATHER enters, half-dressed, without his coat, waistcoat or tie. He hooks his braces

*over his shoulders, shouts, moves round the stage, his hands out
in front of him, groping for the furniture that isn't there.*

FATHER. My tie . . . Oh God in heaven, where's my tie? Will
nobody hand me a waistcoat even? Can't any of you realize the
loneliness of getting dressed?!

The SON *enters with the coat, waistcoat and tie over his arm,
finds the* FATHER'S *wandering hand and puts the tie into it.*

Is that you?

SON. Yes.

FATHER. I suppose you expect me to talk about it.

SON. I know it came as a bit of a shock to you, when Peter
divorced Elizabeth.

FATHER. Must have come as a shock to you too, didn't it? The
fact that she was available for marriage must have rather chilled
your ardour. I mean you're hardly in any state to get married . . .

SON. Do you want to stop us?

FATHER. Are you asking me to? (*Starting to tie his tie without looking.*) How long have you been at the bar, exactly?

SON. Nine months . . .

FATHER. Nine months! I'd been in practise ten years before I felt
the slightest need to marry your mother . . .

SON. Perhaps . . . Needs weren't so urgent then.

FATHER. Got any work have you?

SON. A little work.

FATHER. Unsuccessful defence in a serious case of non renewed
dog licence. That'll hardly keep you in Vim . . .

SON. I don't want to be kept in Vim.

FATHER. But you won't be able to help it – once you're married.
Your no-income will be frittered away on Vim and saucepan
scourers, mansion polish, children's vests and such like
luxuries . . .

SON. I'm quite ready to take on her children.

FATHER. You sound like a railway train. Short stop to take on her children . . . Waistcoat about anywhere? Yes. In the course of her life . . . she has acquired children. Mixed blessings I should imagine, for both of you.

SON. If you're worried about money . . .

FATHER. My dear boy. *I'm* not worried about it. I just think you haven't bargained for the Vim . . . How long are you going to deny me my waistcoat?

SON. Here.

The SON *holds out the waistcoat, helps the* FATHER *to struggle into it.*

I know you think we're insane . . .

FATHER (*buttoning his waistcoat*). You feel the need to be dissuaded.

SON. Of course not. Coat. (*Holding it out.*)

FATHER. I can't help you, you know. (*He struggles into his coat.*)

SON. We don't want help.

FATHER. The children seem lively. As children go. (*Buttoning his coat.*) Of course it won't be I, who has to keep them in rompers! I wonder, should I have a drop of Eau-de-Cologne on the handkerchief? I understand your poor girl's coming to tea. We seem now to be totally surrounded by visitors.

SON. You're not going to be rude to her?

FATHER. Certainly not. Your poor girl and I have got a certain understanding . . .

SON. For God's sake. Why do you keep calling her my poor girl?

FATHER. That's really something . . . I'll have to explain to her after tea.

He takes the SON's *arm. They move off the stage together.*
ELIZABETH *enters. She waits nervously in the garden area: lights a cigarette. The* SON *enters, goes to her quickly, also nervous.*

SON. They're just coming . . . (*Pause.*) It's going to be all right.
(*Pause.*) Whatever he says, you won't mind?

ELIZABETH. Will you?

SON. Of course not.

ELIZABETH. *Whatever* he says?

SON. I'm used to it. (*Pause.*) He doesn't mean half of it.

ELIZABETH. I know. But it's difficult. . .

SON. What?

ELIZABETH. Telling which half he means.

The FATHER *enters in his garden hat, his hand on the* MOTHER'S *arm.*

FATHER. Rhododendrons out?

MOTHER. Yes, dear.

FATHER. A fine show of rhododendrons . . . And the little syringa?

MOTHER. Just out.

FATHER. Just out. And smelling sweetly. Azaleas doing well?

MOTHER. You can see they're a little brown, round the edges . . .

FATHER. Azaleas doing moderately well . . . Our visitor here?

MOTHER. Yes, dear. Elizabeth's here.

FATHER. Is that you?

SON. We're both here.

FATHER. Is your visitor enjoying the garden?

ELIZABETH. Very much. Thank you.

FATHER. Good. And is he treating you well?

ELIZABETH. Quite well. Thank you.

FATHER. I've often wondered about my son. Does he treat girls
well . . .?

SON. Why've you wondered that?

FATHER. I once knew a man named Arthur Pennycuick. Like you
in some ways. He didn't treat girls well . . .

MOTHER. Please, dear . . . Arthur Pennycuick's not suitable.

ELIZABETH. Tell us. What did he do to girls?

FATHER. When I was a young man, I was out with this
Pennycuick. And he picked up a girl. In the promenade of the

old Empire Music Hall. And before he went off with her, he took off his cufflinks and gave them to me for safekeeping. In her *presence*! I felt so sick and angry, seeing him take out his old gold cufflinks. I never spoke to him again. Disgusting!

ELIZABETH. You think if you sleep with someone – you should trust them with your cufflinks?

FATHER. At least not take them out – *in front of the girl*! Well, we can see a fine show of rhododendrons.

MOTHER. Yes. And I showed you the polyanthas.

FATHER. A reward at last, for a good deal of tedious potting up.

ELIZABETH (*impatient, as letting out something she's kept bottled up for a long time*). Why do you bother?

FATHER. What?

ELIZABETH. I said why do you bother to do all this gardening? I mean when you can't see it . . .   •

> *Both the* MOTHER *and* SON *try to interrupt her, protectively.*

MOTHER. My dear . . .

SON. Elizabeth . . .

ELIZABETH. Well he can't see it can he? Why do you all walk about – pretending he's not blind?

> *The* FATHER *shakes off the* MOTHER'S *arm and moves, his hand out in front of him, towards* ELIZABETH. *He gets to her: touches her arm, feels down her arm, and puts his in it.*

FATHER. Is that you?

ELIZABETH. Yes . . .

FATHER. Would you take me to West Copse? I'd like . . . a report on the magnolia. Would you do that? (*Pause.*) Be my eyes.

> ELIZABETH *looks at him, suspicious, not quite understanding what he's up to. Then she says, almost brutally.*

ELIZABETH. Come on then . . .

> *She moves away, with the* FATHER *on her arm.*

MOTHER (*looking after* ELIZABETH). She has nice eyes.

SON. Yes.

MOTHER. Not at all the eyes . . . of a divorced person.

SON. Does he want to stop us?

MOTHER. Well, it's not easy for him. He's such a household word in Probate, Divorce and Admiralty Division.

SON. Is he going on about that?

MOTHER. No. Not at all.

SON. If he could see her he'd understand why I want to marry her.

MOTHER. Oh, he understands that. (*Smiling.*) I think his main difficulty is understanding why she wants to marry you . . .

SON. That's nice of him!

MOTHER (*puts her arm in the* SON's). Would you like to come and help me cut up the oranges? I do hate making marmalade.

SON (*as they move away*). Why not buy it, for God's sake?

MOTHER. He does so enjoy our great annual bout with the marmalade . . .

> *They have now left and the* FATHER *and* ELIZABETH *have arrived at a seat in the garden part of the stage.* ELIZABETH *sits the* FATHER *down and sits down beside him.*

FATHER. Come over, did you, in your own small car?
   Pause.

ELIZABETH. You've been trying to put him off.

> *She moves him towards garden seats. Sits down beside him.*

FATHER. Not at all.

ELIZABETH. I told him. You'd put him off.

FATHER. He came to me for advice.

ELIZABETH. And I suppose you gave it.

FATHER. I never give advice. It's far too precious. Bit of an asset, don't you find, that private transport?

ELIZABETH. We made up our minds.

FATHER. And your children I believe, are pretty lively. For children . . .

ELIZABETH. He gets on marvellously with them . . .

FATHER. And I believe you have your own bits and pieces of furniture. A bedroom suite they tell me. In a fine state of preservation. You're a catch! If you want my honest opinion.

ELIZABETH. Then you ought to be glad for him . . .

FATHER. Him? Look here. Joking apart. You don't want to marry him, do you? I mean he's got no assets . . . of any kind. Not even . . . a kitchen cabinet. And here's another thing about it. (*He takes out a cigar case, removes a cigar.*)

ELIZABETH. What?

FATHER. He won't like it, you know. If you have the flu . . .

ELIZABETH. Really . . .?

FATHER. You see, most people are naturally sympathetic towards illness. They're kind to people with high temperatures. They even cosset them. But not him! He runs a mile. Sneeze once and he'll be off! In the opposite direction!

He puts the unlit cigar in his mouth.

ELIZABETH. I don't get ill all that much . . .

FATHER. But when you do . . . he'll run a mile!

ELIZABETH, I thought it was *me* you might disapprove of . . .

FATHER. Why ever . . .?

ELIZABETH. Think he's marrying someone unsuitable . . .

FATHER. You have particularly nice eyes they tell me.

ELIZABETH. Thanks.

FATHER. And some handsome furniture . . .

ELIZABETH. Not much.

FATHER. And as you told me yourself, your own small runabout.

ELIZABETH. Very bashed.

FATHER. Even so. Not many girls with assets of that description. Couldn't you do better, than someone who bolts if you go two ticks above normal? (*He puts the unlit cigar in his mouth.*)

ELIZABETH. I hadn't thought about it.

FATHER. Oh do think. (*He feels in his pocket, pulls out a box of matches.*) Think carefully! There must be bigger fish than *that* in your own particular sea. (*He strikes a match, holds it some-where in the air.*) You are, I mean, something of a catch.

ELIZABETH *looks at him, smiles, gets up and moves his hand so that the flame lights his cigar.*

You could catch better fish than *that*. I'm prepared to take a bet on it . . . (*He shivers slightly.*) It's getting cold.
ELIZABETH (*gets up, unsmiling*). I'll take you in.

The FATHER *gets up and* ELIZABETH *leads him off the stage. The* SON *enters, wearing a black coat and striped trousers.*

SON (*to the audience*). In that case his advocacy failed. In time he became reconciled to me as a husband for his daughter-in-law.

Pause.

He was right, though. I hadn't bargained for the Vim.

ELIZABETH *enters downstage to the* SON. *She is in a bad mood, stirring something in a pudding bowl.*

ELIZABETH. Made lots of money this week?
SON. Ten guineas. For a divorce.
ELIZABETH. That's marvellous, darling! I had to get them new vests.
SON. What the hell do they do with their vests? In my opinion they eat their vests.
ELIZABETH. And knicker linings. I put them on the account at John Barnes.
SON. The account at John Barnes is assuming the proportions of the National debt.
ELIZABETH. But you ought to be rich.
SON. Ought?
ELIZABETH. I'm up all night. Typing your divorce petitions. They must be paying you – for all those paragraphs of deep humiliation and distress.
SON. You don't get paid for years. In the Law.

ELIZABETH. Can't you ask for it?

SON. Of course I can't.

ELIZABETH. Why not?

SON. You just can't knock on someone's door and say 'What about the ten guineas for the divorce?'

ELIZABETH. I'll go and knock if you like . . .

SON. Anyway, George collects the fees . . .

ELIZABETH. George?

SON. Our clerk. That's his department.

ELIZABETH. He told me his real name's Henry.

SON. My father calls him George.

Light change, upstage a desk. Dim light for the barristers' chambers. GEORGE, *the clerk, dignified, white haired figure with a stiff collar and cuffs comes in, sits down at the desk, opens a drawer, takes out a sandwich and eats.*

ELIZABETH. Whatever for?

SON. Because he once had a clerk called George, who was killed on the Somme . . . So when Henry took over my father went on calling him George.

ELIZABETH. Henry doesn't much like that, if you ask me.

SON. He doesn't mind.

ELIZABETH. You always think no one minds – about your father . .

The SON *moves to her, puts an arm round her shoulder, to cheer her up.*

SON. Let's go to the pub.

ELIZABETH. What on?

SON. The Family Allowance.

ELIZABETH. All right. Shall we play bar billiards?

SON. Like we were doing the night Peter walked in. Remember?

ELIZABETH. And said, 'This is the end of our marriage. I see you've become entirely trivial'.

SON. Do you miss Peter?

ELIZABETH. No. (*Pause, she looks at him.*) Do you?

SON. Of course not.

ELIZABETH. I'm sorry about John Barnes.

SON. That's marriage, isn't it?

ELIZABETH. What's marriage?

SON. An unexpectedly large expenditure on Vim, children's vests and suchlike luxuries . . .

Pause. ELIZABETH *looks at him suspiciously.*

ELIZABETH. Who's that – a quotation from?

Silence. He doesn't answer. They stand for a moment, looking at each other. Upstage, GEORGE *closes the drawer, gets up, takes a hat and umbrella and goes. Downstage* ELIZABETH *and the* SON *go off in different directions; she's still stirring.*

Light change and the SON *re-enters upstage. He looks at the drawers of* GEORGE's *desk. Is tempted. Opens one crack. Peers in. Shuts it when he thinks he hears a noise. Then opens it slowly. Puts in his hand and pulls out a cheque. He looks at the cheque and then whistles with delight. As he is doing so,* GEORGE *re-enters: looks at the* SON *and the open desk drawer and bridles with outrage.*

GEORGE. We have been going, sir, to our personal drawer!

SON. But, George, it's a cheque, for me . . .

GEORGE. We should've given it out to us, sir. In the fullness of time . . .

SON (*kisses the cheque*). Fifteen guineas! Thank God for adultery.

GEORGE. We have never had a gentleman in Chambers that had to grub for money in our personal top drawer . . .

SON. But, George, we're desperately short of Vim.

GEORGE. These things take time, sir.

SON. And what's the point of keeping good money shut up with a box of old pen nibs and a Lyons Individual Fruit Pie. Is it supposed to breed in there or something? (*Pause.*) If you could only get me some more work.

GEORGE. We can't expect much can we? We must wait until a few clients learn to like the cut of our jib.

SON. I've got a talent for divorcing people.

GEORGE. It's not our work. It's our conversation to solicitors that counts. While we're waiting to come on, at London Sessions.

SON. Conversation?

GEORGE. Do we ask them about their tomato plants? Do we remember ourselves to their motor mowers. Do we show a proper concern for their operations and their daughters' figure skating? That's how we rise to heights, in the Law.

SON. My father doesn't do that.

GEORGE. Your father's a case apart.

SON (*rather proud*). My father's obnoxious, to solicitors.

GEORGE (*suddenly shouts*). 'The devil damn thee Black, thou cream faced loon!'

SON (*taken aback*). What?

GEORGE. He said that to Mr Binns, when he'd forgotten to file his affidavit. Your father is something of an exception.

SON. Yes.

GEORGE. I sometimes wonder. Does he realize I'm one of the many Henrys of the world?

SON (*reassuring*). Yes, George. I'm sure he does . . .

Pause. GEORGE *looks at the* SON *more sympathetically.*

GEORGE. Mr Garfield goes down to the Free Legal Centre, Holloway Road. That's where he goes of a Thursday. He picks up the odd guinea or two, on poor persons' cases. And I don't have him in here, sir, ferreting about among my packed meal, sir.

SON. Mr. Garfield lives with his mother – he spends nothing at all on Vim!

GEORGE. He takes the view he might rise to fame from the Free

Legal Centre. He says a murderer might rush in there off the streets any day of the week . . .

Light change. The SON *moves forward and speaks to the audience downstage left. Upstage,* GEORGE *goes. Downstage right, a table and a chair, a portrait of George VI. A* SOCIAL WORKER *with glasses, chain smoking over a pile of files, enters.*

SON. So I went to the Free Legal Centre. To a small room that smelt of old gym shoes and coconut matting where you could hear the distant sounds of billiards and punch ups from the Youth Club and pray that a murderer, still clutching the dripping knife, might burst in from the Holloway Road and beg urgently for Legal Aid.

He turns hopefully to the SOCIAL WORKER.

No murderers in tonight I suppose, Miss Bulstrode?

SOCIAL WORKER. I'm sending you up to my Mr Morrow. I chose you out for him specially.
SON. Why me?
SOCIAL WORKER. He makes Mr Garfield faint.

The SOCIAL WORKER *hands the* SON *a file and goes. The* SON *starts to look at Mr Morrow's file. Change of light upstage and the* FATHER *enters in a black jacket and a light waistcoat, on* GEORGE'S *arm.* GEORGE *sits him down at the upstage desk. The* FATHER *lights a cigar and starts to read a page of braille as the* SON *waits for his Free Legal client.*

SON. Back in Chambers my father, smelling of Eau-de-Cologne and occasional cigars, sat among his relics, the blown duck egg on which a client's will had once been written, the caricatures of himself in great cases, the photographs of the signatures in a notorious forgery. He wrote a great textbook on the law of wills . . . becoming expert in the habits of mad old ladies who went fishing for gold under their beds and left all their money to undesirable causes.

E

FATHER. Let's choose executors and talk of wills.

SON. In the Holloway Road, I waited for more obscure problems.

MR MORROW *comes in downstage to the* SON. *He is an innocent looking, smiling, balding, middle-aged man in a macintosh.*

MR MORROW. Are you the lawyer?

SON. Mr Morrow? Is it matrimonial? (*He opens the file and starts to fill in a form.*)

MR MORROW. Yes, sir. In a sense . . .

SON. You were married on . . .?

MR MORROW. The sixth day of one month. I prefer not to use the heathen notation.

SON. 1940?

MR MORROW. Yes. 1940.

SON. I have to put it down on this form, you see. (*Pause.*) Now – matrimonial offence: I mean, what is the trouble?

MR MORROW. The corpuscles.

SON. There's no place on the Free Legal form for corpuscles.

MR MORROW. Which however, is the trouble . . . That's what I want, sir. The legal position . . . She's on to the red ones, now. I could just about stand it when she only took the white. And my child, sir. My Pamela. I have a very particular respect for that child, who is now losing her hearty appetite.

SON. What's your wife doing exactly?

MR MORROW. She is eating our red corpuscles.

SON. If you're feeling unwell, Mr Morrow. . .

MR MORROW. She drains them from us, by the use of her specs. That is how she drains them out. She focuses her rimless specs upon our bodies, and so our bodies bleed.

SON. Mr Morrow. . .

MR MORROW. I was standing upon the hearth rug, sir, which lies upon my . . . hearth. I looked down between my legs and I saw it there. The scarlet flower. There was the stain of blood on my white fleecy rug sir, red between my legs.

Pause.

SON. Have you spoken to your wife about this at all, Mr Morrow?

MR MORROW. I haven't spoken to her, sir. But she is forgiven. All the same I feel she has let me down. When it was the white she trained her eyes on, sir, it was more or less immaterial. But now she's after my vital strength.

SON. Legally . . .

MR MORROW. A man stands entitled to his own blood, surely. It must be so.

Pause.

SON. I know of no case actually decided, on this particular point.

MR MORROW (*eager*). You're advising me to go to Doncaster, then?

Pause.

SON. You . . . might as well.

MR MORROW. It's your considered and expert opinion, her destructive eye won't be upon me in Doncaster?

SON. Why not try it anyway?

MR MORROW. Very well, sir. I bow to your honest opinion. I shall discontinue all legal proceedings and proceed to Doncaster. Will you require my signature to that effect?

SON. Well, no. I hardly think so.

MR MORROW. That's as well, as it so happens. I never sign, for ethical reasons. (*He moves away.*) It's not the blood I miss, sir. It's the child we have to consider. With all due respect.

He goes. The SON *is left alone. He closes the file and puts it down on the table. Upstage the light increases on the* FATHER *upstage. He repeats loudly.*

FATHER. 'Let's choose executors and talk of wills!'

The SOCIAL WORKER *comes in downstage to the* SON.

SOCIAL WORKER. Mr Morrow looks well contented.

SON. He should. He has absolutely no need of the Law.

The SON *and the* SOCIAL WORKER *go off downstage left.*

FATHER. 'And yet not so . . . For what can we bequeath?
Save our deposed bodies to the ground.
Our land, our lives and all are Bolingbroke's.
And nothing can we call our own but death
And that small model of the barren earth . . .

The SON *enters upstage, hangs up his hat.*

That serves as paste and cover to our bones.'
. . . You're back from lunch.

SON. Yes.

FATHER. You took a long time.

SON. I was talking to a man – he might want to put on my play . . .

FATHER. Possibly you'd work harder if you were a woman
barrister.

SON. Possibly . . .

FATHER. I've often said to George, 'Let's have a woman in
Chambers'. Women *work* so much harder than men, they can be
imposed on so much more easily. Look how seriously girls'
schools take lacrosse! They'd treat the law like that. I could get
a ridiculous amount of work from a woman pupil.

SON. What does George say?

FATHER (*sad.*) He says there's not the toilet facilities . . . But you
know old Carter Davidson once had a woman pupil. He occu-
pied the basement here, rooms easily visible from the garden
where the Masters of the Bench stroll, after dinner. Well, they
were strolling there, history relates, after a Grand Night with
some kind of Royal Personage, King, Queen, Princess . . .
something of the kind, and glancing down, what did they see?

SON. Well – what?

FATHER. Carter Davidson and his woman pupil! Naked as
puppies, stretched out on the Persian rug. Well, not a word was
said, but do you know?

SON. What?

FATHER. Next day Sir Carter Davidson was appointed Chief Justice of the Seaward Isles. They shipped him off, ten thousand miles from the Inns of Court. He couldn't ever understand why. (*Laughs.*) Well, that's one way to get a blooming knighthood . . . Enjoying the Law, are you . . . ?

SON. Not all that much.

FATHER. Plays are all very well. Photographs in the paper may be all very fine and large. But you need something real! Hold hard on the law.

SON. Are you sure the Law's real?

FATHER. What on earth do you mean?

SON. No one seems to need it . . . except lawyers . . .

FATHER. The law's not designed for imbeciles, or your friends who combine the art of being called Bill with membership of the female sex. It's not exactly tailor made for the poet Percy Bysshe Shelley . . . No! The whole point of the Law is – it's designed for the ordinary everyday citizen seated aboard the ordinary, everyday Holborn tramcar.

SON. I don't think they have trams in Holborn any more.

FATHER. That's hardly the point.

SON. No trams and no ordinary commonsense citizen sitting on them or anywhere else in the world. They're all busy thinking of the things that really worry them, like the shapes on the ceilings and the stains on the carpet, and they only pretend to be ordinary commonsense citizens when they need lawyers. It's a disguise they put on, like the blue suits and old Boy Scout buttons and the terrible voice they use to take the Bible oath. They're deceiving you, that's what they're doing. They think if they play your game we'll let them off their debts, or order their wives to permit them sexual intercourse, or liberate them from old pointless crimes no one holds against them anyway. All that commonsense legal language we're so proud of – I tell you honestly, it might as well be Chinese . . .

FATHER (*conciliating*). Oh, well now . . . You can get a lot of innocent fun out of the Law. How's your cross?

SON. What?

FATHER. Your cross examination. In Court – have you the makings of a cross examiner?

SON. I don't know.

FATHER. Timing is of great importance. In the art of cross examination.

SON. That's show business.

FATHER. What did you say?

SON. An expression, used by actors.

FATHER (*without interest*). Really? How interesting. Now I always count, in silence of course, up to forty-three before starting a cross examination.

SON. Whatever for?

FATHER. The witness imagines you're thinking up some utterly devastating question.

SON. And are you?

FATHER. Of course not. I'm just counting. Up to forty-three. However, it unnerves the gentleman in the box. Then, start off with the knock out! Don't leave it till the end; go in with your guns blazing! Ask him . . .

SON. What?

FATHER. Is there anything in your conduct, Mr Nokes, of which, looking back on it, you now feel heartily *ashamed*?

SON. Is that a good question?

FATHER. It's an excellent question!

SON. Why exactly?

FATHER. Because if he says 'yes' he's made an admission, and if he says 'no' he's a self-satisfied idiot and he's lost the sympathy of the Court.

SON. Anything else?

FATHER. Say you've got a letter in which he admits something discreditable . . . like, well having apologised to his wife for instance . . . Now then, how're you going to put that to him?

SON. Did you, or did you not . . .

FATHER. Not bad.

SON. Write a letter apologising to your wife?

FATHER. Well, I suppose you're young.

SON. Isn't that right?

FATHER. Not what I should call the *art* of cross examination.

SON. So how . . .?

FATHER. You be Nokes.

SON. All right.

FATHER. You behaved disgracefully to your wife, did you not?

SON. No.

FATHER. In fact, so disgracefully that you had to apologise to her.

SON. I don't remember.

FATHER. Will you swear you did not?

SON. What?

FATHER. Will you swear you didn't apologise to her?

SON. All right.

FATHER. Now please turn to the letter on page 23. Just read it out to us will you?

SON. I see. (*Pause*). What's the point of all this actually?

FATHER (*standing up, very positive*). The point. My dear boy, the point is to do down your opponent. To obliterate whoever's agin you. That's what the point of it is . . . And of course, to have a bit of fun, while you're about it.

Tapping with his stick, the FATHER, *feels his way off. The* SON *moves down stage and speaks to the audience.*

SON. My father got too old for the train journey to London . . .
A ROBING ROOM MAN *comes in with a wig and gown, stand up collar and bands, and stands by the* SON. *As he speaks the* SON *unfixes his own collar, hands it to the man, takes the collar which is handed to him, puts it on, ties the bands and is robed in the wig and gown. Upstage Courtroom arches are projected, a* JUDGE *is sitting in wig and gown. A* LADY WITNESS, *in a flowered hat and gloves is waiting to be questioned.*

My father retired on a pension of nothing but credit, optimism and determination not to think of anything unpleasant. His money had gone on cigars and barrels of oysters and Eau-de Cologne for his handkerchief and always first class on the railway and great rare Japanese cherry trees that rustled in the wind and flowered for two weeks a year in a green-white shower he never saw. He left to me all the subtle pleasures of the law . . .

JUDGE (*loudly to the* SON). Do you want to cross examine this witness?

SON (*turns round as if woken from a reverie and enters the Court-room scene*). Certainly, my Lord.

JUDGE. Very well, get on with it.

SON (*turns to the witness*). Now madam . . .

WITNESS. Yes.

SON (*starting on a menacing pause, he begins to count under his breath*). One . . . two . . . three . . . four . . . five . . . six . . . seven . . . eight . . . nine . . .

JUDGE. Are you intending to *ask* any questions?

SON. Twelve . . . thirteen . . . I'm sorry, my Lord . . .?

JUDGE. If you've got a question to ask, ask it. We can't all wait while you stand in silent prayer you know.

   Offstage, sound of laughter.

SON. I'm sorry my Lord . . . Now, madam. Is there anything you've ever done you're ashamed of?

WITNESS. Yes.

SON. Ah. And what're you ashamed of?

WITNESS. I once wrote up for an autograph . . . with picture. You know the type of thing. At my age! Well I began off 'Am heartily ashamed to write up but –'

JUDGE. Have you any *relevant* questions?

SON. Will you please read this letter? The one I am about to hand you . . .

WITNESS. Oh, yes.

SON. Read it out to us, please.

WITNESS. I can't . . .

SON. Madam. The Court is waiting . . .

WITNESS. I really can't.

SON. Is there something there you'd rather not remember?

WITNESS. Not exactly . . .

SON (*very severe*). Then read it, madam!

WITNESS. Could I borrow your glasses?

Laughter.

The laughter fades. Light change as the SON *goes. The* MOTHER *is laying the dinner table. The* FATHER'S *in his arm chair, his eyes closed, apparently asleep. A small table with a portable radio on it.* ELIZABETH *enters, exhausted from putting the children to bed. She and the* MOTHER *talk quietly, not to wake up the* FATHER.

MOTHER. Are the children settled?

ELIZABETH (*lighting a cigarette*). Yes. They're all settled.

MOTHER. How's our little Jennifer?

ELIZABETH. Your little Jennifer's fine. (*She starts to help her lay.*) And so are our Daniel and Jonathon.

MOTHER. Jenny's so pretty. I'd like to have done a drawing of her. Perhaps a crayon . . .

ELIZABETH. Why don't you?

MOTHER (*laughs at the ridiculousness of the idea*). Oh, I gave up drawing when I got married. You have to don't you – give up things when you get married . . .

ELIZABETH. Do you?

MOTHER. And of course there's no time now . . .

ELIZABETH (*looks at the* FATHER *and whispers*). Doesn't he leave you half an hour to yourself?

MOTHER (*whispers*). He doesn't like to be left. I suppose . . . I often think. (*She pauses with a handful of cutlery.*) Someday I'll be alone shan't I. You can't help thinking.

Pause. ELIZABETH *looks at her.*

F

ELIZABETH. (*whispers*). What'll you do? Travel. Go to France.

MOTHER. Oh no. I shall stay here of course. Somebody has to see to the marmalade.

> *She puts down the handful of cutlery and determinedly goes on laying. Sound of a car stopping.* ELIZABETH *looks out, as if from a window.*

ELIZABETH. There he is – come to join the family for the week-end.

MOTHER. It seems they're giving him a lot of briefs now.

ELIZABETH. Yes.

MOTHER. It's hard to believe. (*Pause.*) It must be keeping you very busy.

ELIZABETH. Me? Why me?

MOTHER. Don't you help him – with his cases?

ELIZABETH. He's got a secretary now. He hardly ever discusses his work: he thinks I take it too seriously.

MOTHER. Of course his father misses going to London – He used to get such a lot of fun, out of the divorces . . .

FATHER (*opening his eyes*). What's that?

MOTHER. I said you missed going to London, dear.

FATHER. It's my son, you know. He's pinched all my work.

> *The* SON *enters carrying a bottle of champagne.*

SON. Victory!

ELIZABETH. What's happened, darling?

SON. I won . . . Timson *v* Timson. After five days.

FATHER (*smacking his lips*). Five refreshers!

SON. They insisted on fighting every inch of the way. Terribly litigious . . .

FATHER. The sort to breed from – those Timsons!

SON. I brought champagne. For a small celebration.

> *He starts to open the champagne.*

ELIZABETH (*mutters*). Just like a wedding.

SON. What did you say?

ELIZABETH. Oh nothing.

SON (*pours a glass of champagne. Gives it to the* MOTHER).
Champagne . . .

MOTHER. How festive. Isn't it festive, dear?

The SON *is handing a glass to the* FATHER.

FATHER. What is?

MOTHER. He's handing you a glass of champagne.

FATHER. I'm glad you can afford such things, old boy. Now that
you've pinched all my practice. (*He drinks.*) I suppose you're
polite to solicitors?

SON. Occasionally.

FATHER. I could never bring myself . . . Pity. If I'd gone to dinner
with solicitors I might've had something to leave you – over and
above my overdraft. I remember after one case, on The Temple
Station, my solicitor said, 'Are you going West, dear boy, we
might have dinner together'. 'No' I lied to him, I was so
anxious to get away. 'I'm going East.' I ended up with a sandwich in Bethnal Green. It's been my fault . . . The determination
– to be alone. (*He drinks.*) You know what'd go very nicely with
this champagne?

MOTHER. What, dear – a biscuit?

FATHER. No. The crossword.

The MOTHER *sits beside the* FATHER *and opens* The Times. *The*
SON *pours champagne for* ELIZABETH. *She turns on the radio,*
they drink. The radio starts to play an early Elvis Presley. The
SON *and* ELIZABETH *start to dance together : a slow jive.*

MOTHER. The N.C.O. sounds agony.

FATHER. How many words?

MOTHER. Two. Eight and ten.

FATHER. Corporal Punishment.

MOTHER. How clever!

FATHER. Oh, I've got this crossword fellow at my mercy.

ELIZABETH. You're very clever, darling.

SON. Yes.

Pause.

ELIZABETH. The only thing is . . .

SON. What?

ELIZABETH. I thought . . . I mean in that Timson *v* Timson. Weren't you for the husband?

SON. Of course I was for the husband.

ELIZABETH. Wasn't he the man who insisted on his wife tickling the soles of his feet. Four hours at a stretch . . .

SON. It was only while they watched television.

ELIZABETH. With a contraption! A foot tickler . . .?

SON. Something he improvised. With a system of weights and pulleys. It was ingenious actually. The work was done with an old pipe cleaner.

Pause.

ELIZABETH *(Puzzled). Ought* he to have won?

SON *(correcting her). I* won.

ELIZABETH. But *ought* you . . .?

SON. The Judge said it was part of the wear and tear of married life.

ELIZABETH. Yes, but how did *they* feel about it. I mean, I suppose they're still married, aren't they?

SON. They looked a little confused.

ELIZABETH. Perhaps they didn't appreciate the rules of the game.

SON. I enjoyed it . . .

The music stops. They stand facing each other.

ELIZABETH. You enjoy playing games?

SON. I . . . I suppose so.

ELIZABETH. You know what?

SON. What?

ELIZABETH *(quite loudly)*. You get more like him. Every day.

The FATHER *looks up.*

FATHER. Isn't it time we had dinner?

MOTHER. It's all ready.

She moves with the FATHER to the table. From the other side of the stage the SON and ELIZABETH move towards the table.

ELIZABETH. Will he try and start arguments at dinner?

The FATHER and MOTHER sit down at the dining table.

SON. Of course.

ELIZABETH. Why?

SON. Because that's what he enjoys.

They sit down at the table too. An awkward silence, which the FATHER breaks.

FATHER. Music! I can't imagine anyone actually *liking* music.

Pause.

The immortality of the soul! What a boring conception! Can't think of anything worse than living for infinity in a great transcendental hotel, with nothing to do in the evenings . . .

Pause.

What's the time?

MOTHER. Half past eight.

FATHER. Ah! The time's nipping along nicely. (*Pause.*) Nothing narrows the mind so much as foreign travel. Stay at home. That's the way to see the world.

ELIZABETH. I don't know that's true.

FATHER. Of course it's true! And I'll tell you something else, Elizabeth. Just between the two of us. There's a lot of sorry stuff in D. H. Lawrence.

ELIZABETH. I don't know about that either.

FATHER. Oh yes there is. And a lot of damned dull stuff in old Proust. (*Pause.*) Did you hear that, Elizabeth? Lot of damned dull stuff in old Proust.

ELIZABETH. Yes. I heard.

FATHER. I'll say one thing for you . . . At least you're an improvement on the ones he used to bring home. Girls that would closet themselves in the bathroom for hours on end. And nothing to show for it . . . None of them lasted long.

ELIZABETH. I wonder why?

FATHER. Yes. I wonder. At least my son's someone to talk to. Most people get damned dull children.

> *The* SON *fills his glass. The* FATHER *puts his hand out, feels the* SON's *hand.*

Is that you?

SON. Yes.

FATHER. Your play came across quite well they told me.

SON. Yes.

> *Pause.*

MOTHER. Won't you have one of my little tarts?

> *Pause.*

FATHER. I see that other fellow's play got very good notices. You want to watch out he doesn't put your nose out of joint.

> *Pause.*

I haven't been sleeping lately.

> *Pause.*

And sometimes when I can't sleep, you know, I like to make a list of all the things I really hate.

MOTHER. Do have one of my little tarts, Elizabeth.

ELIZABETH. Is it a long list?

FATHER. Not very. Soft eggs. Cold plates. Waiting for things. Parsons.

SON. Parsons?

FATHER. Yes. Parsons. On the wireless. If those fellows bore God as much as they bore me, I'm sorry for Him . . .

ELIZABETH. My father's a parson.

FATHER. I know. (*Pause.*) 'Nymph, in thy orisons be all my sins remembered.'

Pause. He smacks at the air with his hand.

Is that a wasp?

MOTHER. Yes, dear.

FATHER. What's it doing?

MOTHER. It's going away.

FATHER. After you've been troubled by a wasp, don't you love a fly?

Pause.

Don't the evenings seem terribly long now you're married? Aren't you finding it tremendously tedious? What do you do – have wireless?

ELIZABETH. We don't get bored, exactly.

SON. We can always quarrel.

FATHER. I was surprised to hear about that play of yours.

SON. Were you?

FATHER. When you told us the story of that play, I said 'Ha. Ha. This is a bit thin. This is rather poor fooling'. Didn't I say that?

MOTHER. Yes, dear.

FATHER. 'This is likely to come very tardy off.' But now it appears to have come across quite well. Didn't that surprise you, Elizabeth?

ELIZABETH. Well . . .

SON. She doesn't like it.

FATHER. What?

SON. Elizabeth doesn't like it very much.

FATHER (*interested*). Really? That's interesting. Now tell me why . . .

Pause.

ELIZABETH. Not serious.

FATHER. You don't think so? You think he's not serious.

ELIZABETH. He plays games. He makes jokes. When the time comes to say anything serious it's as if . . .

SON. Oh for heaven's sake!

FATHER. Go on.

ELIZABETH. There was something stopping him. All the time . . .

FATHER. Is that true? I wonder why that is . . .

ELIZABETH. I should think you'd know.

FATHER. Why?

ELIZABETH. Because you've never really said anything serious to him, have you? No one here ever says anything . . . They make jokes . . . and tell stories . . . and . . . something's *happening*!

SON. Elizabeth. It doesn't always have to be said.

ELIZABETH. Sometimes. Sometimes it has to.

FATHER. All right. What would you like to hear me say? What words . . .of wisdom?

Silence. They look at him. No one says anything. Very softly he starts to sing.

FATHER (*sings*). 'She was as beeootiful
            As a butterfly
            And proud as a queen
            Was pretty little Polly Perkins
            Of Paddington Green . . .'

The SON *gets up from the table and moves forward towards the audience. Light fades on the upstage area, where the* FATHER, MOTHER *and* ELIZABETH *go.*

SON (*to the audience*). He had no message. I think he had no belief. He was the advocate who can take the side that comes to him first and always discover words to anger his opponent. He was the challenger who flung his glove down in the darkness and waited for an argument. And when the children came to see him he told them no more, and no less, than he'd told to me . . .

THREE CHILDREN *run in. Two boys and a girl, dressed in jeans*

and sweaters. They take packets of mints out of the FATHER's
*waistcoat pocket, pull out his gold watch, blow on it and he makes
it open miraculously for them.*

FATHER. Who's this?

GIRL. Daniel . . .

FATHER. Oh really. And you're . . .

FIRST BOY. I'm Jennifer . . .

GIRL. I'm Daniel. Honestly.

SECOND BOY. She's a liar.

FATHER. Oh come now. If she says she's Daniel – shouldn't we
take her word for it?

FIRST BOY. Tell us some more . . .

FATHER. What about?

SECOND BOY. The Macbeths . . .

GIRL (*with relish*). The Macbeths!

They sit down, look up at him. The FATHER *starts to tell the
story. The* SON, *downstage, looks on.*

FATHER. Dunsinane! What a dreadful place to stay . . . for the
weekend. Draughts. No hot water. No wireless! The alarm bell
going off in the night just when you least expected it. And
finally . . . The dinner party!

CHILDREN. Go on! Tell us! Tell us about the dinner party!
(*etc.*)

FATHER. A most embarrassing affair. Dinner with the Macbeths.
And everyone's sitting down . . . quite comfortable. And his
wife says 'Come and sit down, dear. The soup's getting cold . . .'
And he turns to his chair and sees . . . (*He points with a trembling,
terrible finger.*) Someone . . . Something, horrible! Banquo . . .
(*His voice sinks to a terrifying whisper.*)

'The time has been
That, when the brains were out the man would die,
And there an end; but now they rise again
With twenty mortal murders on their crowns,

And push us from our stools . . .'
He grabs the GIRL *by the arm. The* CHILDREN *are roaring with laughter.*

SON. I used to scream when he did that to me.
The CHILDREN *become quiet again. The* FATHER *is talking to them, telling them stories. They are listening.*

(*To the audience.*) His mind was full of the books he read as a boy, lying in the hot fields in his prickly Norfolk Jacket. He told them about foggy afternoons in Baker Street and sabres at dawn at Spardau Castle, and Umslopagas and Alan Quartermaine and She Who Must Be Obeyed. He spoke to them of the absurdities of his life . . .

FATHER. My old father was a great one for doing unwelcome acts of kindness! Recall his rash conduct in the affair of my Uncle George's dog . . .

During this story which the CHILDREN *know by heart, they prompt him.*

FIRST BOY. It's the dog . . .!
SECOND BOY. Go on about the dog.
GIRL. Uncle George's Dog . . .
FATHER. My poor Uncle George fell on evil days . . . and had to sell his faithful pointer. And my father, thinking he was heart-broken, went furtively about . . . to buy the animal back. It was a most . . .
GIRL. Lugubrious hound?
FATHER. With a long powerful rudder! It seldom or never smiled. It was not so much dangerous as . . .
FIRST BOY. Depressing?
FATHER. Depressing indeed! And as soon as he saw it, my Uncle George went off to Uxbridge where he had taken a post with good prospects and diggings at which animals were unfortunately not permitted . . . He shed no tears, to my old father's

surprise, at parting from his dumb friend who then took up
residence with us. (*He starts to laugh.*) A most ...

GIRL. Unwelcome guest ...'

FATHER. Now at that time my brother conducted evening classes.
In Pitman's shorthand! And the dog used to crouch at the
corner of the house by night and when my brother's pupils
arrived he foolishly mistook them for burglars and sprang out at
them! Our house happened to be built on a sort of low cliff, and
more than one of the students dropped off the edge of the cliff
and was (*Laughing loudly.*) badly hurt!

> *Upstage* ELIZABETH *enters, stands looking at the* FATHER *and
> the* CHILDREN.

ELIZABETH. We must get back. We must really.

CHILDREN. No, Mummy. It's the one about the dog ... Let's
finish the dog. (*etc.*)

FATHER (*laughing, the* CHILDREN *begin to laugh with him*). My
brother's shorthand lessons became unpopular. (*Laughs.*) We
offered the dog to anyone who'd provide a good home for it.
Then we said we'd be content with a thoroughly bad home for
the dog. (*Laughs.*) We offered the dog to anyone who'd provide
a good home for it. Then we said we'd be content with a
thoroughly bad home for the dog. (*Laughs.*) Finally we had to
pay the owner a large sum of money to take the animal back.
(*Laughs.*) But my mother and I used to remember terrible
stories – about faithful hounds who were able to find their way
home ... (*He laughs uncontrollably as the* CHILDREN *pull him to
his feet and join him in shouting the last line of the story.*)

FATHER AND CHILDREN. *Over immense distances!*

ELIZABETH. Come on now. We must go, really.

> *The* MOTHER *comes in, takes the* FATHER's *arm. They stand
> waving as* ELIZABETH *and the* CHILDREN *go off, shouting
> 'Goodbye', 'Goodbye'. Then when* ELIZABETH *and the*
> CHILDREN *have gone, the* FATHER *and* MOTHER *turn and go
> on the other side of the stage.*

*Light change. Projection of the garden. Weedy and overgrown.
Sound of wind.*

SON. The enormous garden became dark and overgrown in
spreading patches. He continued, every day, to chronicle its
progress in the diary he dictated.

Offstage voice, amplified, the FATHER *speaks.*

FATHER. Put sodium chlorate on the front path. We had raspberry
pie from our own raspberries. The dahlias are coming into
flower. The jays are eating all the peas . . .

SON. Willow herb and thistles and bright poppies grew up. The
fruit cage collapsed like a shaken temple and woods supported
the tumbled netting. The rhododendrons and yew hedges grew
high as a jungle, tall and dark and uncontrolled, lit with un-
expected flowers . . .

FATHER (*O.S.*). Thomas came and we saw him standing still
among the camellias . . .

SON. A boy was hired to engage the garden in single combat. His
name was not Thomas.

FATHER (*O.S.*). Planted a hundred white crocus and staked up
the Malva Alcoa. A dragon fly came into the sitting room.
Thomas was paid. Am laid up. The pest officer arrived to
eliminate the wasp nests. Unhappily I couldn't watch the
destruction . . .

SON. In the summer, with the garden at its most turbulent, he
became suddenly very old and ill . . .

ELIZABETH (*O.S.*). 'What are you going to take for breakfast,
Mr Phelps?' said Holmes, 'Curried fowl, eggs or will you help
yourself?'

Change of light upstage. The FATHER *is in bed.* ELIZABETH *is
sitting at his bedside, reading to him. On the other side of the bed,
there is an oxygen cylinder and a mask.*

ELIZABETH. 'Thank you, I can eat nothing,' said Phelps. 'Oh
come. Try the dish before you.' 'Thank you, I would really

rather not.' 'Well then' said Holmes, with a mischievous twinkle 'I suppose you have no objections to helping me?'

The FATHER *is gasping, breathing with great difficulty.* ELIZABETH *goes on reading.*

'Phelps raised the cover, and as he did so, uttered a scream, and sat there staring with his face as white as the plate upon which he looked. Across the centre of it was lying a little cylinder of blue-grey paper . . .'

FATHER (*gasps*). The Naval Treaty!

ELIZABETH. Yes.

FATHER. I'm afraid . . . you find that story a great bore.

ELIZABETH. Of course not. It was very exciting.

FATHER. Dear . . . Elizabeth. I'm so glad to discover . . . you can lie as mercifully as anyone . . .

The SON *moves upstage to the bed.* ELIZABETH *gets up and goes. The* SON *sits down beside the bed. Pause. The* FATHER's *breathing is irregular. Then, with a sudden effort, he tries to get out of bed.*

I want a bath! Get them to take me to the bathroom. Cretins!

The SON *holds him. Pushes him gently back into bed.*

SON. Lie still. Don't be angry.

FATHER (*back in bed, gasping*). I'm always angry – when I'm dying.

His breathing becomes more irregular. Stops altogether for a moment when the SON *grabs the oxygen mask and puts it on his face. There's a sound of loud, rasping, regular, oxygen-assisted breath. The light and projections change to night.*

SON. It was a hot endless night, in a small house surrounded by a great garden in which all the plants were on the point of mutiny.

Long pause. The breathing continues. The SON *gets up, stands, looks down at his* FATHER *who is now sleeping. The* DOCTOR *comes in. He is in a dinner jacket. He nods to the* SON *and leans over the* FATHER.

SON. Dr Ellis . . .

DOCTOR. We've got a territorial dinner. In High Wycombe . . .

SON. How is he?

DOCTOR. Wake up! Wake up! (*To* SON.) Don't let him sleep. That's the great thing. Wakey wakey! That's better . . .

SON. But do you think . . .?

DOCTOR. The only thing to do is to keep his eyes open. There's really nothing else. I've spoken to your mother. (*Pause.*) I'll come back in the morning.

The DOCTOR *goes. The* SON *turns back to the bed. Looks at the* FATHER. *Sits on the bed and speaks urgently.*

SON. Wake up! Please! Please! Wake up!

The oxygen breathing mounts to a climax and stops. Silence. The SON *gets up slowly. Slowly the light fades upstage and, as it is in darkness, the* SON *moves downstage and speaks to the audience.*

SON. I'd been told of all the things you're meant to feel. Sudden freedom, growing up, the end of dependence, the step into the sunlight when no one is taller than you and you're in no one else's shadow.

Pause.

I know what I felt. Lonely.

He turns and slowly walks away. The stage is empty. And then becomes brilliantly lit, the back wall covered with projections of the garden in full flower.

THE END

Methuen's Modern Plays

EDITED BY JOHN CULLEN

*   *   *